"Vogler's *The Writer's Journey* is the Bible for screenwriters. I think it's the best book on how to write a screenplay ever written. It helped me get through so many roadblocks as a writer. Vogler's approach to screenwriting was based on Joseph Campbell's theory that, because of myths, the arc of a hero's journey was a story ingrained deeply inside all of us. I really incorporated his ideas and techniques into how I structured films—I referred to it a lot."

> — Darren Aronofsky, Academy Award–nominated director of
> *Black Swan*

"Story structure is 90% of the game in screenwriting, though it's invisible on the page. Great movies have great structure — period. Nobody understands that better, and communicates it more brilliantly, than Mr. McKenna. His insight is a key reason I'm a working writer today."

> — Mark Fergus, Oscar-nominated co-screenwriter, *Children of*
> *Men* and *Iron Man*

"Just finished reading *Memo from the Story Dept.* (so I could write this blurb) and it's already saved my ass. I needed to come up with a pitch for a rewrite and this book helped me figure out a way to crack it. No shit."

> — Scott Silver, screenwriter (*8 Mile*, Oscar-nominated for *The*
> *Fighter*)

"The way that Vogler and McKenna tag-team this book — it keeps you on your toes. Sometimes when you're yelling in the wilderness, it's good to have two voices. Certainly they'll give you perspectives on screenwriting that you've never seen before — and in this world of multiple screenwriting book choices, that's a good thing."

> — Matthew Terry, filmmaker/screenwriter/teacher, columnist
> for *www.hollywoodlitsales.com*

"Make no mistake: this book is completely inaccurate. Why? Because no story department has ever given notes this good. This book is such a wonderful walk through story, theme, and character that every writer — and development exec — should keep a copy on their desk."

> — Chad Gervich, writer/producer (*Wipeout, Reality Binge,*
> *Speeders, Foody Call*), author of *Small Screen, Big Picture:*
> *A Writer's Guide to the TV Business*

"With his encyclopedic recall of movies, plays, novels, et al., David McKenna offers real-world examples to guide the writer through the murky morass that is screenwriting. He's funny, insightful, and makes the impossible mission of writing a great script feel (dare we hope?) possible."

— Susan Dansby, Emmy Award–winning television writer, author of *How Did You Get That Job?*

"There are at least two sides to every good story, and when it comes to writers grasping an element in the storytelling craft, it can take two or more points of view sometimes to really understand it. Chris and David accomplish giving you many new perspectives and that 'aha' feeling of clarity. They get you started with the 'Want' List, things that drive you through life and your characters through your story (without a driver, no one goes anywhere). *Memo from the Story Dept.* is highly recommended for all writers who wish to gain the focused attention of their audience, one of the rarest and most valuable commodities of all time."

— Ann Baldwin, screenwriter (*The Power of Dreams*)

"Co-written by Christopher Vogler and David McKenna, this is a book that deserves a spot on any writer's shelf, as well as providing a nice companion to Vogler's previous book, *The Writer's Journey*. The style in which *Memo from the Story Dept.* is written (chapters from each author and short critiques on each other's ideas) is fresh and interesting to read."

— Erin Corrado, *www.onemoviefiveviews.com*

"*Memo from the Story Department* is a deeply human exploration of the art of sharing life through movie stories. This book is a profound and inspirational road map. But it uses humor, heart and creativity to open us to its messages. A fantastic must-read for all screenwriters."

— Pen Densham, Hollywood producer/writer/director including *Robin Hood Prince of Thieves*, *Moll Flanders* and over 300 hours of TV including the *Outer Limits* and *Twilight Zone* revivals

MEMO
FROM THE STORY DEPT.
SECRETS OF STRUCTURE AND CHARACTER

For Michael
All the best
on your creative quest

CHRISTOPHER VOGLER

&

DAVID McKENNA

Chris Vogler

CHARLESTON 2015

Published by Michael Wiese Productions
12400 Ventura Blvd. #1111
Studio City, CA 91604
tel. 818.379.8799 | fax 818.986.3408
mw@mwp.com | www.mwp.com

Cover design: Johnny Ink *www.johnnyink.com*
Interior book design: Gina Mansfield Design
Illustrations: Michele Montez and Fritz Springmeyer
Editor: Paul Norlen

Printed by McNaughton & Gunn, Inc., Saline, Michigan
Manufactured in the United States of America

Library of Congress Cataloging-in-Publication Data

Vogler, Christopher, 1949-
 Memo from the story department : secrets of structure and
character / Christopher Vogler and David McKenna.
    p. cm.
 ISBN 978-1-932907-97-1
 1. Motion picture authorship. 1. McKenna, David, 1949- II.
Title.
 PN1996.V62 2011
 808.2'3--dc22
                                        2011003012

Mixed Sources
Product group from well-managed
forests and other controlled sources
www.fsc.org Cert no. SW-COC-002283
© 1996 Forest Stewardship Council
FSC

Dedication
— Vogler —

For Alice, *cara mia*

Dedication
— McKenna —

For Jie...

Table of Contents

ACKNOWLEDGMENTS

 VOGLER

I would like to make grateful acknowledgment to my many great teachers, Sister Angelique Dryden and others at St. Dominic High School, and to Dave Johnson, Mel Sloan, Dick Harber, Mort Zarkoff, Drew Casper, Wolfram von Hanwehr, and Irwin Blacker at the USC School of Cinema Arts.

Many thanks to Fritz Springmeyer for his artistic insights and advice.

 McKENNA

I owe an unpayable debt to the many teachers, classmates, colleagues and students who have helped shape me and the contents of this book. Foremost among them is Annette Insdorf who has graciously provided me a professional home as a teacher at Columbia University's School of the Arts. I can't begin to list the theatre artists who have collaborated with and inspired me over the years, but I must note Jaston Williams and Joe Sears who have helped me make a living in the trade. I am deeply grateful to my friend Susan Dansby for her suggestions and editorial input. Finally, I'd like to thank my mother and my sister for their patience and willingness to play.

INTRODUCTION

———— VOGLER ————

The tools and techniques in this volume are the result of many years of spirited debate and collaboration between myself, Chris Vogler, and my friend and colleague David McKenna. Both of us do many jobs, but most of our careers we have been professional story analysts, meaning that we read and evaluate stories, screenplays, and novel manuscripts for the story departments of major movie studios. Between the two of us we estimate we have critiqued over forty thousand stories in one form or another, plus working together on dozens of writing projects.

In order to do this work, we have had to build up an inventory of terms and concepts to describe what we're dealing with: essential elements of stories such as structure, character, and theme. We've asked a lot of questions and made up our own theories and language to manage this unruly subject, but we are just the latest in a long line of questioners stretching all the way back to Aristotle. We are grateful for the work of our predecessors, and want to set down in this book some of the things we learned from them, along with our own insights and interpretations. And then we'll hand it over to you in the hope that you will find the mysteries of story as fascinating as we have, and that you will continue to ask these questions and add to the body of knowledge.

THE TOOL KIT

We think of this book as our mental tool kit, a collection of essential instruments that extend our reach, improve our aim and efficiency, and make our craft much easier. There are many kinds of tools in these pages, tools for defining characters, laying out structures, determining themes, clarifying intentions, and intensifying the pleasure of the audience.

Those who have read my book *The Writer's Journey: Mythic Structure for Writers* know that I based my approach to designing and troubleshooting stories on the work of the great mythologist Joseph Campbell (1904-87). I adapted his work into a twelve-stage outline of the typical "Hero's Journey" narrative structure as expressed in movies, and attempted a theory of character archetypes based on work done by Campbell and the Swiss psychologist Carl Jung.

Useful though they are, Hero's Journey structure and archetypes are only two among many instruments in the storyteller's tool box. In my daily work with stories I reach for many other tools such as the legacy of vaudeville and the theatre, the traditional wisdom of Hollywood, the know-how of Walt Disney, the language of psychology, as well as principles borrowed from music, dance, painting, martial arts, architecture, and the military. David has other tools acquired in his training and experiences as an actor, singer, voice-over performer, acting coach, pickup basketball player and theatrical director. And we both bring to the tool kit everything we learned at the greatest school of all, the Academy of Hard Knocks.

In these pages we will share with you what we consider to be the essential principles and techniques for creating good stories.

So, what is in this tool kit we are offering?

First, we will give you the essential tools of structure, character, and theme. I will briefly review the twelve-stage structural model of the Hero's Journey and the gallery of character possibilities embodied in the eight major Archetypes, tools covered in a deeper way in *The Writer's Journey*. I will expand on structure and character with some new material, describing tools that I've used for years but never written about until now, such as Vladimir Propp's analysis of Russian fairy tale structure and a clever little book on character types written by Aristotle's follower Theophrastus. David will introduce the powerful tools of Polar Opposites, Reciprocal Action, and The Want List, all basic storytelling equipment. We'll have something to say about the essential story department tools of Log Line and Synopsis, and how they can help any storyteller clarify themes, characters and intentions.

A major section of the book will be David's presentation of something he calls the Six Environmental Facts, which is a way of looking at characters and entire stories through six different prisms: the economic, social, religious and political conditions in the story as well as the influence of time and place. David's exploration of these Environmental Facts is a development of a method for analyzing plays and preparing scenes pioneered by a University of Texas professor, Francis Hodge.

Taken together, these six environmental factors build up a complete, multi-dimensional picture of the subject, allowing actors and directors to make informed choices that will express the theme more dramatically. We believe they can be equally useful for screenwriters and producers of theatrical films, for designers of games and interactive media, or for anyone wishing to harness the full power of stories.

The book will close with David's suggestion that you make a Five-Year Plan, and I will have a few words of encouragement before unleashing you upon the world to make better stories.

One thing we both feel strongly about: None of this will make sense or be worthwhile unless you put it to work. More than a tool kit, you might think of it as a well-equipped garage waiting for cars that need to be repaired or customized. We have found that when you put a theory to the test, when you apply some principle to a particular work, there is a strong payoff that seems to defy the laws of physics, returning more energy than you invested. Try it for yourself; take any of the tools in this book and apply them to a movie you've seen, a book you've read, or a project you are working on, and you will find a surprising amount of energy will be released. You will only truly possess these tools once you have put them to work; until then they are just theories.

So go ahead, make the most of it, and add your own experiences to the legacy of storytelling.

My Time in the Story Department

———— McKENNA ————

I have never wanted to write a book. Christopher Vogler made me do it.

By nature, I am a troubadour, a gadfly, a raconteur, an entertainer. I fell into directing plays and was a carefree young fellow, traveling from one low-paying gig to another. I was learning lessons about showmanship and my craft, and I was happy to ply my trade for anyone willing to pay the piper.

Then I met Mr. Vogler, who is a far more serious and determined gent than I. Aside from his snarky wit, what attracted me to him was his unique ability to read obscure tomes and to distill their arcane information into digestible and tasty nuggets of wisdom. Gadfly meets Harry the Explainer.

We shared an insatiable appetite for stories and how they are made.

Being serious, Chris applied himself to getting steady work in the film industry. Aware that I was inclined to gig forever, Chris took me in hand and insisted that I join him.

He showed me how to make a living as a reader/story analyst for film studios. On one level, he was being kind to a penniless fool. On another, he was recruiting a comrade to help decipher the lessons his artistic journey was revealing and a colleague who would provide different lessons for him to consider. Over a very long time on the job, we have analyzed uncounted thousands of screenplays. We have been and remain a two-man story department.

So this book (which I never wanted to write) is an artifact of our four-decade conversation. The son of an amateur handyman whose claim to fame was canoes constructed from concrete, Chris is on a lifelong mission to describe how things work and to create a better set of tools. *The Writer's Journey* and his chapters within this book are fruits of that search.

He's badgered me for years to explain what I know. He finally handcuffed me to a keyboard and got his wish. If my contribution to this book proves to be half as valuable to storytellers and audiences as Chris' work has been, I'll be a very happy man.

Who Are Those Guys?

Butch Cassidy: *They're beginning to get on my nerves. Who are those guys?*
— from the screenplay *Butch Cassidy and the Sundance Kid*
by William Goldman

Early versions of Vogler (left) and McKenna trying to figure it all out at the La Purisima Mission in Lompoc, California (photo by Joyce Garrison)

I am a farm boy from Missouri; David is a product of the suburbs of New Jersey. So how did these two guys get thrown together to begin their odyssey in the country of storytelling?

When I was about twelve years old my family moved from the suburbs of St. Louis to a farm forty miles west of the city. As a kid I was fascinated by movies, fairy tales, myths and legends, comic books, anything with a story. I knew I wanted to be in the story game somehow. I studied broadcast journalism at the University of Missouri and, after graduation, joined the U.S. Air Force. As a young officer I was sent to Los Angeles to make documentary films about the military space program, then after a couple of years was transferred to Kelly Air Force Base in San Antonio, Texas to make training videos.

I had an interest in theatre and acting, and went downtown with one of my friends from the base to try out for a part in a local production of *Dial M for Murder*. My friend said the director was an interesting character, a rising star and a rebel in the local theatre scene by the name of David McKenna.

McKenna was indeed a colorful character, with long hair, unruly beard and the loud voice of a kid from New Jersey. Boiling over with energy, he was constantly bouncing a rubber ball or twirling a cane. His manner was brash and vulgar but very funny, and his unorthodox taste as a director appealed to me. He reminded me of Bugs Bunny, irreverent, mischievous but good-hearted.

David cast my friend, a much better actor than me, in a major role and gave me a small part as a policeman. Because I was good with accents, I also provided several radio and telephone voices needed for the production, and tried to make myself useful by volunteering to "keep book," that is, following along in the script as we went through rehearsals, writing down all of the director's notes. David became very stern and unforgiving as he assumed the director role, taking full control of the theatre and everyone in it. He knew exactly what he wanted and didn't seem interested in anyone else's opinion.

By the standards of the day his directorial choices were exotic, daring, challenging to the audience. But it was clear he had reasons for his choices, some principles he was following. He dealt in the language of movies, speaking of shots, angles and cuts and using classic films as references. His taste in movies and his pleasure in them seemed to overlap with mine. I wanted to jump in and make comments, but kept silent, trying to write down everything he said.

Then David was on his feet staging the big action scene of the play, a struggle in which a woman being attacked by a murderer turns the tables in self-defense, stabbing him to death with a pair of scissors. David finished blocking the scene and was about to move on, but I suddenly found myself blurting out "What if he's not dead?!"

McKenna turned to look at me, his eyes wide. The first thought on his face was "Who the hell is this guy interrupting the flow of my directing?" and the second was "Hey, that's a good idea!"

"He's like a vampire," I dared to continue. "She kills him, the audience buys it, she buys it. But then he jumps up — he's not dead! He comes after her again, with a pair of scissors sticking out of his back! She has to kill him all over again!"

David liked the idea and immediately incorporated it into the play. That evening, after the rehearsal, we went to a coffee shop and began the decades-long discussion that is the fabric of this book.

We discovered that we had a lot in common, born a few months apart in one of the peak years of the baby boom, 1949, both growing up in sprawling middle-class families with a certain amount of ethical orientation drummed into us by the Catholic church. We shared an appreciation for Western movies and an interest in history and the supernatural. But most of all, over time, we seem to share most the love of story in all its forms. We learned that we had some facility at it, a natural sense of structure, and a vast array of examples in our mental inventory.

We became friends and worked together on several stage shows in San Antonio when the theatre scene in that town was remarkably vibrant and creative. It was a magical time when it seemed we could do anything. Like all such times it had to come to an end and the creative spirits who had gathered briefly there dispersed to the four winds. The end of the magic coincided with the end of my tour of duty in the Air Force. Both David and I sensed that we needed to know more about the crafts we wanted to pursue, and so we split up to go to graduate schools on opposite sides of the country, though we promised to keep the creative spark alive by staying in touch.

David headed East to Carnegie-Mellon in Pittsburgh to hone his skills as a theatre director, while I returned to Los Angeles to gain more skills in writing and directing for film, going to the USC Cinema School on the G.I. Bill.

I was looking for something in those days, an organizing principle or general theory to make sense of the seemingly chaotic world of story. Looking back, I see that David may have already found his version of a Unified Field Theory for storytelling, in the approach to directing he had learned in his undergraduate training at the University of Texas at Austin, from Professor Hodge. I found mine a little later, at USC, when a professor introduced me to the world of Joseph Campbell and the Hero's Journey concept, a life-changing experience that led to the writing of *The Writer's Journey* and formed the foundation of my career.

Through those years and beyond, David and I did keep in touch. In fact we worked at it quite seriously. In long letters we compared notes on the training we were getting and the new movies that were coming out. After graduate school, David started directing theatre and coaching actors while I got my first jobs as a story analyst in Hollywood. We still managed to get together for a few days every year for intense sessions of analyzing movies and discussing the stories we encountered in our work. But there was something deeper going on, a search for the hidden structure of it all.

I was finding steady work in Hollywood as a story analyst, reading scripts and stories and writing reports on them called "coverage." I was good at it and earned a reputation for being good with structure, in part because of the tools that the Hero's Journey put in my hands. One year when David was visiting me in Los Angeles I introduced him to the story editor at 20th Century-Fox where I was working. He said there might be work for David in the New York office of the Fox story department and encouraged him to prepare some samples of coverage to display his story analysis skills.

Then, as David remembers it, I put him through a hellish course of training, making him rewrite his sample coverage countless times before it was ready. But apparently it was worth the effort, for he got the job and has been in demand as a skilled story analyst ever since.

After a couple of years I left the Fox story department for a new job at Disney, which had just gone through a drastic change of management and corporate culture and was newly energized. I got a little deeper into the mysteries of the movie development process, doing historical research, writing reports on various aspects of popular culture, and composing detailed notes on screenplays being prepared for production.

I never lost sight of my interest in the deep storytelling principles, in the unwritten rules of story logic, especially the patterns of structure and character I'd found in Campbell's Hero's Journey model. The urge built inside me to put down my thoughts about the model's huge potential as a guide to movie storytelling. I wanted to write it up into a short, useful statement of the basic principles in the form of a studio memo, the kind that Disney production chief Jeffrey Katzenberg had famously used to spell out marching orders for the new Hollywood.

I decided to take time off from work to focus on the project and flew to New York to bounce my ideas off David. We worked together intensely for over a week, discussing and testing every aspect of the pattern, tugging and adjusting the language here and there. David was extremely helpful with thinking of classic movie examples to illustrate the thousand possible variations on the Twelve Stages.

When we had worn out his VCR looking at old movies, I went back to L.A. to write up the memo that I called "A Practical Guide to the Hero with a Thousand Faces," the famous or infamous seven-page structure guide that soon began infiltrating Hollywood story culture. (You'll find it reproduced in Chapter 6.)

I sent the first copy to McKenna, and then started handing it out to my story analyst friends and to key Disney executives. "Interesting," was all that most people said, at first. But I knew, I sensed somehow, that I was on to something. I had the vision that copies of The Memo were like little robots, moving out from the studio and into the jet stream of Hollywood thinking, all on their own. Fax machines had just been invented and I envisioned copies of The Memo flying all over town, and that's exactly what happened.

Feedback suggested I had hit a nerve. I heard young executives buzzing about it, telling their friends about it. It became the "I have to have it" document of the season at talent agencies and in studio executive suites like that of Dawn Steel at Paramount. In the sincerest form of compliment, it was plagiarized, with more than one ambitious young executive putting his name on the cover sheet and claiming it as his work. You really know you're onto something when somebody thinks it's worth stealing.

Here's one of those places where the Hero's Journey and the archetypes come in handy in real life. I recognized that those plagiarizers were just Threshold Guardians, like the "false claimants" who pop up in the fairy tales to say that they, not the hero, slew the dragon. The hero must pass another test to claim his reward. And so I did a daring thing, writing a letter to Jeffrey Katzenberg who had praised The Memo at a staff meeting. I claimed to be the true author of the document and requested a boon — greater involvement in story department decision-making.

He granted my wish, sending me to work with Disney Feature Animation, which was just getting back on its feet after a long period of decline since Walt Disney's death. When I arrived I found The Memo had preceded me, and the animators were already outlining their story boards with Hero's Journey stages.

The Memo served as a handout when I began teaching story analysis at the UCLA Extension Writers' Program. It grew to twelve or fourteen pages, as I developed the ideas more fully and added more examples. Eventually I included material about the archetypes and soon there was enough material to contemplate a book, and thus *The Writer's Journey* was born from a humble seven-page acorn.

Meanwhile, David and I continue to meet up once a year or so to watch old movies and share what we've learned from our story department work and our personal reading interests. We collaborate on writing projects and never seem to lose interest in all the amazing things there are to learn about stories. He's turned out to be a terrific teacher as I always suspected he would be, and he keeps surprising me with his insights about movies, stories, and life.

One day we realized we had been talking and thinking about stories for so long that it made sense to write this book, and so it came to pass. Now let's open up the tool kit and see what's inside.

CHAPTER ONE

You Gotta Have a Theme

VOGLER

When you are developing a story, one of the most important and fundamental questions you have to ask yourself is "What is my theme?" Theme is a tool that can help you focus your work, making it a coherent design organized around a single idea or human quality that is explored in every scene.

What is your story about, really? Not in the sense that Macbeth is about a Scottish lord who kills a lot of people to become king, but in the sense of a single word that defines the emotional arena of the story. According to playwright Lajos Egri, who wrote about it in *The Art of Dramatic Writing*, the theme of *Macbeth* is *ambition*, the drive to dominate.

You often hear actors and directors say things like "Our story is about" x, y, or z when they are being interviewed about their new movies and TV shows. They say it's about trust, mercy, betrayal, friendship, or ruthlessness, but whatever word they choose can tell you a lot about their story. That's because they've all thought long and hard about the tale they've told, until they can boil it down to its essence.

Words like "theme" and "premise" are used interchangeably, but let's say for our purposes of story discussion that a theme is a one-word statement of some human drive or quality that runs as a unifying factor all the way through the story. And let's say that a premise is a more developed articulation of that theme, turning the one word into a short sentence that specifies what the creators think about that feature of humanity. One form it can take is almost like a mathematical equation: X behavior leads to Y consequences.

Theme (from Greek) means something set down, a proposition or a deposit. Premise (from Latin) means something sent ahead, or again a proposition. A premise in logic is a proposition, a statement, set down first in a chain of ideas, on which all the other ideas will depend.

If the theme of *Macbeth* is ambition, then Shakespeare's premise is that a certain kind of ambition, ruthless ambition, leads inevitably to destruction. The play unfolds to prove that point, scene by scene.

Macbeth himself doesn't see it that way, not until it's too late. The premise on which he runs his life is "Ruthless ambition leads inevitably to being king." It's a clear instance of the story trying to teach the eternal lesson, "Ask not for what you want but for what you really need." He could have chosen another premise, such as "Selfless ambition, tempered by mercy, leads to a long and happy reign." Instead, he wanted to be king at any cost, not realizing it would ultimately cut him off from the rest of humanity and seal his doom.

I'm generally in favor of a clear statement of a theme or premise in a line of dialogue somewhere early in the first act. It might be a wish spoken aloud by the hero, or an opinion about life offered by another character. The hero might accept it or challenge it, but it will resonate throughout the rest of the story. It will hang as a question over the subsequent scenes. It will be challenged in every possible way and we will get to explore many arguments for and against the proposition. If one character comforts a heart-broken lover with the premise statement, "Don't worry, love conquers all," then that idea will be battered with all kinds of counter-arguments from characters who cynically believe love is a trap or a delusion of fools. At the end, we'll return to the premise, perhaps rephrasing it to reflect what we've learned, or simply repeating it, but with much deeper understanding because of the lessons the story has taught us about that particular human quality.

The theme or premise may not be stated so openly. In some scripts it may only drift into our consciousness through the repetition of certain words, phrases or situations. I once had the assignment of rewriting an action script that seemed to have no perceivable theme or premise. There was no dramatic or emotional level to the story, only a sequence of action scenes. I struggled along for seventy pages of the rewrite until I noticed that a certain word of dialogue was recurring in the mouths of different characters, in lines I'd written like "I don't trust my instincts anymore," "You'll have to trust me on this one," and "How do we know we can trust you?" It dawned on me that "trust" could be a good theme for this movie, about an untested young woman officer suddenly thrown into a combat situation. I immediately went back to the first scene and re-conceived it as being about trust, showing how the young woman didn't trust her own instincts. I continued through the script, trying to find some way to explore the theme of trust in every scene. I decided the premise was that "Learning to trust yourself leads to being trusted by others." Alas, that movie never got made, but I'd had my first experience of seeing how a script becomes more textured and dramatically interesting when unified by a theme and premise.

Knowing the theme and premise makes a whole series of aesthetic choices easier and clearer. If you know the essence of the story, what it's really about, you know what moods and feelings you are trying to create, and thus what colors to paint the set, what pace to keep, what kind of music to use. The work begins to feel organic, coherent, interconnected, and purpose-ful, more like a living being organized around a common spine and central nervous system.

Feel free to change your mind during the development process about the story's true theme and premise. That may not emerge clearly until the story is well along, and your first thoughts about it may or may not end up reflecting the true essence of the story as it evolves. But at some point the writer or director must commit to a theme and premise, and from then on the whole script or production should fall into line to support the argument of the play, allowing the audience to join in evaluating all sides of a given human condition.

What can we say is the theme of The Wrestler, *with its lonely anti-hero who tries to make a go of a normal life but decides it's his true nature to go out in a heroic blaze of glory? Some have said Redemption; maybe it's Integrity: To thine own self be true. What do you think?*

SOMETHING TO THINK ABOUT

What is the one-word theme of your life? What is your one-sentence premise? Is there anything you'd like to change?

What is the one-word theme of your favorite movie or novel? What is its one-sentence premise? Does it expand on the one word, expressing a strong point of view about that human quality?

NOTE FROM McKENNA

Since this book is a two-hander, I'm going to chime in occasionally to comment on Chris's contributions and he will do the same for mine.

Like Chris, I am frequently hired by screenwriting clients to provide critical feedback. Applying the "theme" tool helps me build immediate trust and provide a path forward. When my client knows I understand his/her story on the fundamental level, we have a point of rapport and a launching pad for the re-write process.

Recently a lawyer-turned-screenwriter had me analyze his script about a groundbreaking case he'd argued. His screenplay masterfully described the issues of law, but it felt more like a thoughtful documentary than an emotionally compelling drama.

When we sat down to discuss all this, I told him that his law case had engaged me intellectually but left me hungry for emotional involvement. I needed a tasty theme. We started talking about the themes of our favorite lawyer films (memories of *Anatomy of a Murder*, *Erin Brockovich* and *The Verdict* popped up) and deduced that those movies worked emotionally because the legal arguments had been spiced with transcendent personal stories.

Would the corporate pollution case in *Erin Brockovich* matter to us if it didn't include the thematic collision between trailer trash Erin and her upscale, uptight colleagues? David Mamet posits a good case of medical neglect in *The Verdict*. But his story stays with us because a boozy defense lawyer is fighting the uncaring system to redeem his very soul.

My client and I were sniffing out this sort of theme when he mentioned something amazing. He admitted that handling the case introduced him to a level of responsibility that he'd never experienced before. Bingo!

Could this theme of responsibility exist in all the threads of the script? Indeed it could. In fact, that theme seemed to be waiting at all points to see if we'd be smart enough to find it. Bingo, Part Two!

Once we enticed our theme out of its hiding place, our new approach took care of itself. The script would no longer be a mere play-by-play about a legal question: it became a series of dramatic showdowns forcing the characters to confront their personal responsibilities for the conditions of their lives.

Within a few weeks, my client completed a new draft: a taut legal thriller about a groundbreaking lawsuit that transforms the lives of almost everyone involved in it. We used a very simple tool to elevate fact into drama.

CHAPTER TWO

THE "WANT" LIST

McKENNA

"There are three rules to writing, and nobody knows what they are."
— W. Somerset Maugham

This is a quote from one of the twentieth century's best storytellers, and I use it to keep myself humble as a teacher. I don't know how anyone creates art. It's a mystery that requires inspiration, hard work and something indefinable that can't be learned by following rules from a book (I can hear my publisher groaning).

Thankfully, craftsmanship (if not artistry) can be taught. It has hard rules that become malleable under an artist's touch. So a wise artist goes through "basic training" with those rules before toying with them.

However, it seems to be the way of the world that uninitiated would-be artists dive right in without submitting to this "basic training" in craftsmanship.

My drama school classmates and I were not particularly wise in the matter of training. We were acting students, filled with passionate impulses and skeptical about the need for wisdom. We would perform scenes for our teacher, filled with youthful brio and good intentions. Most of our work was pretty crappy.

Having suffered through our work, that teacher would begin each critique session with a simple question: "What does your character want?" Dozens of scenes would be performed throughout the semester, and the question was posed every single time. Without fail, the response was a lot of hemming and hawing from us students. We were pretty hilarious in our insistent ignorance.

It's a legacy that continues. I've taught my share of acting classes and have seen hundreds of acting scenes. As my teachers did before me, I almost always ask: "What do you want here?" As I and my classmates did decades ago, my students look at their shoes and mumble something along the lines of "I dunno."

So, in the name of basic training in craftsmanship, I want you and I (mostly you) to make up a list of "wants." Since we know that the question will be asked every single time, we will look like "A" students if we at least have some sort of answer.

So, what do people "want"? We can start with the basics: food, clothing, shelter. Can we make up a story about these basic desires? I don't see why not. Isn't the desire for all three the issue that drives the heroes of Blake Edwards' *Victor/Victoria*?

We can open things up from there. Alcoholics want booze; just ask Nicholas Cage from *Leaving Las Vegas*. Sinners want redemption. Almost all of us yearn for love and recognition. *Braveheart's* William Wallace laid it all on the line for freedom and, after all these years, Mick Jagger still can't get no satisfaction.

In case we've forgotten, Cyndi Lauper informs us that girls just want to have fun.

In fact, pop songs are a virtual textbook of "wants." The kids from *Fame* "want to live forever." Aretha wants R-E-S-P-E-C-T, and in *Some Like It Hot*, Marilyn Monroe wants to "be loved by you, just you and nobody else but you." In Marilyn's case, it looks like a sweet yen. But give it to Glenn Close in *Fatal Attraction*, and the simple "want" gets downright scary.

Michael Corleone wants family, and he's willing to kill to secure it. That's his tragedy, right? How many of us just yearn for a mate and kids? What dramatic action would we take to acquire such things?

It's probably not polite to say so, but most of us are willing to make damned fools of ourselves to fulfill our sexual "wants." And how about the supporting character in Mary Chase's comedy *Harvey* who just wants to sit under a tree with some beer and a girl who pats his hand saying "there, there"? It doesn't seem like much, but it feeds an entire "B" plot.

Money drives most of us to some degree or other, and James Bond wouldn't have much to do unless an endless stream of bad guys wanted to dominate the world. James himself seems satisfied with a bottomless supply of exotic cigarettes, devastating femme fatales and martinis shaken, not stirred. Come to think of it, I want those things, too.

Sports teams want to win championships, and hundreds of films record what they sacrifice to accomplish it.

Almost every Broadway musical opens with an "I want" song. It's the anthem declaring the hero's desire that will be shaped and tested by the ensuing action. Belle from *Beauty and the Beast* musically yearns for a life of adventure like the ones in the books she reads. Eliza Doolittle from *My Fair Lady* wants a "loverly" room somewhere with one enormous chair. The song "Omigod You Guys" from *Legally Blonde* tells us that Elle Woods wants to marry Warner, and the rest of the story chases that desire.

Are there more "wants"? I have to think so. Career advancement, honor, recognition, victory, home, world peace, friendship, serenity, solitude, knowledge, wisdom, insight, answers, communion with God. The list goes on and on, and every item on it could be the foundation for a solid story.

For us as storytellers, the "want" list becomes a primary device to be continually sharpened and kept near at hand in our craftsman toolbox. A story doesn't even get started until somebody wants something and moves in a direction to get it. Your writing has an immediate advantage if you have a character "want" at your fingertips.

Just to be helpful, I asked a group of my recent students to build a "want" list with me. I'll attach it below. But get to work on your own personal list, too. Once you've got it, put it in your toolbox and put it to work.

Love
Money
Pleasure
Validation (Approval)
Security
Revenge
Stability
Power
Victory
Freedom
Acceptance
Fame
Redemption
Respect
Adventure
God
Truth
Justice
American Way
Change
Attention
Peace
Sex
Happiness
Family
Immortality
Communication
Survival

Knowledge
Wisdom
Drugs
Escape
Good Story
Talent
Stability
Certainty
Home
Normalcy
Excitement
Inspiration
Fun
Independence
To Forget
To Remember
Legacy
Progress
Forgiveness
Friendship
Death
Fashion/Beauty
Control
Identity
Company/Companionship
Solitude
Adrenaline/Rush
Rock 'n' Roll (see Drugs, Sex)

NOTE FROM VOGLER

I sat in on one of David's Columbia classes recently and joined him and his students in critiquing screenplay scenes they had written. Over and over we had the same question: What does this character want? Until that is determined, scripts and scenes seem wishy-washy, disorganized, and spineless.

I have my own version of the Want List, a hierarchy of things that drive us through life. We may not realize it but we are all running our lives according to certain prime directives, chosen from a standard list of wishes that exist in every person to some degree. Each person, and each character in a story, consciously or more often unconsciously, has chosen from the list one drive that commands his behavior above all others. Other drives are present in descending order of importance, but one drive usually dominates. For example, above all, I must have my way, I must be inconspicuous at all costs, I must always have the last word, I must be seen as having a lot of money, I must feel secure and in control at all times, I must be different from everyone else, etc.

Stories seem to be interested in these choices, and often set out to force a protagonist to consciously re-assess that habitual, unconscious hierarchy of drives. At the end of the story, someone who put the drive to win above all may come to edit the list, bringing another drive to the fore like the need for love or friendship. In my own life, my prime directive for many years was "Everyone must like me," which meant that I must never do anything to upset anyone, and must please others even at the expense of harming myself. The story of my life has conspired to teach me a lesson — the desire to please others is a good quality in its proper place but it's a lousy way to run your entire life. I've learned to be happy with myself and let other people love me or hate me as they choose.

CHAPTER THREE

What's the Big Deal?

VOGLER

Hollywood is a sink-or-swim industry where they rarely take time to teach you anything, but I got a useful lesson early in my career when I was a reader for Orion Pictures. Our story editor called a meeting of the readers to tell us none of us had any idea what a scene was. I was surprised; I thought I knew. A scene is a short piece of a movie, taking place in one location and one span of time, in which some action takes place or some information is given. Wrong, she said.

And proceeded to explain that a scene is a *business deal*. It may not involve money but it will always involve some change in the contract between characters or in the balance of power. It's a transaction, in which two or more people enter with one kind of deal between them, and negotiate or battle until a new deal has been cut, at which point the scene should end.

It could be the overturning of a long-established power structure. The underdog seizes power by blackmail. The people rise up against a dictator. Someone tries to leave a relationship or overcome an addiction.

Or it could be the forging of a new alliance or enmity. Two people who hated each other make a new deal to work together in a threatening situation. A boy asks a girl out and she accepts or rejects his offer. Two gangsters make an alliance to rub out a rival. A mob forces a sheriff to turn a man over for lynching.

The meat of the scene is the negotiation to arrive at the new deal, and when the deal is cut, the scene is over, period. If there's no new deal, it's not a scene, or at least it's not a scene that's pulling its weight in the script. It's a candidate either for cutting or for rewriting to include some significant exchange of power.

The story editor pointed out that many writers don't know what a scene is, either, and put in non-scenes that are just there "to build character" or to get across exposition. They don't know when to begin and end a scene, wasting time with introductions and chit-chat and dragging the scene out long after the transaction has been concluded. The scene is the deal. When the deal is done, get off the stage.

I found this principle very useful in pinning down the essence of a scene, and I found it also works at a macro level for identifying the bigger issues in a script, for every story is the re-negotiation of a major deal, a contract between opposing forces in society. Romantic comedies are a re-negotiation of the contract between men and women. Myths, religious stories, and fantasies rework the compact between humans and the greater forces at play in the universe. The terms of the uneasy balance between good and evil are re-evaluated in every super-hero adventure and story of moral dilemma. The climax of many movies is a courtroom judgment that lays out a new agreement, passing sentence on a wrongdoer, proclaiming someone's innocence, or dictating terms of a disputed transaction. In all situations, we go in with one deal and we come out with a new deal having been cut.

Knowing when the big deal of the movie has been cut tells you when the movie should be over. Many movies today go on long after they have truly ended, as far as the audience is concerned. They know it's over when the last term of the deal has been decided, and they get restless if the filmmaker goes on with extra flourishes and codas and flash-forwards to ten years later, etc. When I was a kid going to drive-in movie theatres I noticed many people starting their engines and driving away before the last movie of a double bill was quite over. For them the deal of the whole movie was complete when the monster was killed or the murderer was caught, and they didn't need to stick around to see the hero kiss the girl and ride off into the sunset. "When the deal is done, get off the stage" is a good rule for scenes and for the overall structure of stories as well.

NOTE FROM McKENNA

One of my perks for being a "friend of Vog" is access to unexpected eruptions from his volcanic brain. His thought-bombs are sporadic and unpredictable. Sometimes they subject me to long and winding treks down the bottomless rabbit hole. But more often than not, they point me to the mother lode.

"What's the Big Deal" is pure gold. I got it in the mail one morning, and I immediately jettisoned my lesson plan for that afternoon's screenwriting class. I printed up the memo, snatched a random video from the library and presented both to my students.

With the memo in mind, we began to watch the DVD and instantly pinpointed the scenes which were working and those that dragged. We had a new diagnostic tool to add to our storytelling gear! From that point and for the rest of the semester, we discussed student scenes in terms of "deals." The level of writing got a whole lot better.

Chris doesn't name the Orion story editor who caught and shared this nugget, but let me toss a few kudos in his/her direction…

Reply from Vogler: For the record, her name was Migs Levy and she deserves those kudos. Whatever kudos are.

CHAPTER FOUR

The Contract
with the Audience

—————— VOGLER ——————

If a scene is a deal, then what is a story? One answer is that a story, too, is a deal, but the contract in this case is not between characters in a scene but between you and your audience. The terms are these: They agree to give you something of value, their money, but also a much more valuable consideration, their time. As a screenwriter you are asking them to pay attention to you *and you only* for ninety minutes, and as a novelist for much longer. Think about that! Focused attention has always been one of the rarest and most valuable commodities in the universe, and it's even truer today, when people have so many things fighting for their attention. So for them to give you even a few minutes of their focus is huge stakes to put on the table, worth much more than the ten bucks or so they shell out for a book or a movie ticket. Therefore, you'd better come up with something really good to fulfill your part of the bargain.

There are many ways to fulfill that contract with the audience. I used to think the "Hero's Journey" model that I describe in my book *The Writer's Journey* was the whole contract, and an absolute necessity. I still think it is the most reliable way to honor the terms of the deal with the audience, providing them with a cathartic metaphor for their lives that includes a taste of death and transformation. They tend to read it into any story anyhow, and it's actually hard to find a story that doesn't display some of its elements. But I've come to see it's not the only way to hold up your end of the deal.

At a minimum you must be entertaining, that is, able to hold their attention with something a little novel, shocking, surprising, or suspenseful. Be sensational; that is, appeal to their sensations, give them something sensual or visceral, some experience that they can feel in the organs of their bodies, like speed, movement, terror, sexiness.

Laughter is another way to fulfill the contract with the audience. People are so starved for laughter that a movie that makes you laugh out loud a few times is probably going to be a hit. They'll overlook a stupid or pointless story if the movie delivers on the laugh clause in the contract. They didn't go to see movies about Francis the Talking Mule in the 1950s for the heart-warming, thought-provoking Hero's Journey stories, and they don't expect Alvin and the Chipmunks to change their lives.

A good ride to another place and time can fulfill the contract. I don't remember much of the story of *The Abyss* but I felt well repaid by being taken to a cool dark place under the sea for two hours on a hot summer afternoon. James Cameron is great at creating entire worlds, the elegant world of *Titanic*, the ravishing world of *Avatar*, and his movies are rewarded with success because they satisfy the "take me to another place" part of the contract so well.

Giving the audience stars they like in appealing combinations is a way the studios have always used to fulfill the contract with the public. Breathless movies trailers used to proclaim: "You loved Tracy and Hepburn in *Adam's Rib*; here they are together again in *Pat and Mike!*" Putting beloved stars into different costumes is another way to satisfy the entertainment contract. You thought Russell Crowe looked good in the gladiator kit; you'll love him in the Robin Hood outfit.

Sheer novelty weighs heavily with audiences, justifying the investment of their time and attention. It's worth a lot to people to be able to talk about the movie everyone's buzzing about, be it *Psycho*, *The Crying Game*, *Pulp Fiction*, *The Blair Witch Project*, *The Passion of the Christ* or *300*. To fulfill that clause of the contract, there'd better be something really strange, scary, shocking, thrilling or surprising inside that movie so that people can talk about it knowingly after they've seen it.

One of the most powerful ways to honor the terms of the entertainment contract is to fulfill a deep wish held by many members of the audience — to see the dinosaurs walk again in *Jurassic Park*, to fly and wield superpowers in *Superman*, to be seduced by sexy teen vampires in the *Twilight* series. Walt Disney realized that fairy tales were driven by wishes and built his brand identity around giving people the wholesome fantasy experiences they wanted, filled with wish-granting fairy godmothers, wizards and genies.

Up in the Air *fulfilled the contract in several ways, with appealing, complex charac- ters and good story, but really scored by catching something in the zeitgeist. (I also have to love this movie for highlighting the futuristic design of the Lambert Field terminal building in St. Louis. My Dad helped build those concrete arches.)*

Sometimes a movie fulfills the contract by simply cap- turing something in the zeitgeist, the prevailing mood of the moment. Movies will sometimes accidentally line up with a cur- rent issue. Famously *The China Syndrome*, dealing with a fictional nuclear plant meltdown, was released within days of the Three Mile Island nuclear accident and became the movie everyone wanted to see. *Up in the Air* had good performances and story but it also happened to be released, after many years in preparation, just as many Americans found themselves thrown out of work and so its story of corporate gunslingers flying around to fire people struck a chord. Of course a movie can also be killed by current events. After the 9-11 attacks on the U.S. a number of movies were shelved because they featured tall buildings being attacked and destroyed. That was not the way people wanted to have their contract fulfilled at that moment.

At first I resisted the idea that it's all wheeling and dealing — it can't just be about business, can it? But I came to see it is, in a way. From the Bible on down we have lived by our contracts, for the Bible is an account of the covenants or deals made between God and his creation. We all have an unwritten deal with the rest of society, called the social contract, to behave ourselves in return for our freedom and relative safety. The essential documents of our civilization are contracts, agreements made or statements declaring the terms of a new deal, from Hammurabi's Code and the marriage contract to the Bill of Rights. Just be sure when you tell your story that you've thought about "What's the deal going down here?" in every scene and "What's the big deal?" of the whole story. Think of the attention and time your clients, your audience, have put on the table, and try to fulfill your part of the bargain with something that at least entertains them, grants their wishes, perhaps stimulates and amuses them, and maybe even transforms them a little bit.

NOTE FROM McKENNA

Annette Insdorf is my boss at Columbia University. A few years ago, she asked me to create a 14-week course in Auteur Studies. I was stumped for a second about which auteur to choose until I realized that producer-director-composer-movie star-icon Clint Eastwood's astoundingly long career hadn't been discussed at Columbia. He became our topic.

The class was scheduled to begin in a few weeks when Annette bumped into Mr. Eastwood at an industry function. When she mentioned our plans, he responded with his trademark squint and sweetly growled, "Don't let him bore the kids."

Now *that's* a contract with the audience (and very likely the key to Clint's status as a filmmaking legend).

CHAPTER FIVE

Polar Opposites

—— McKENNA ——

The other day, I had a student writer present the beginnings of an idea during a workshop session. She featured two sisters who are basically in tune with each other at the outset and who remained so throughout.

This was as far as she'd gotten, and she was frustrated that she couldn't find the story. So I asked her to consider the differences, rather than the similarities, between the characters.

I was asking her to use the storytelling tool of Polarities, of Polar Opposites.

Responding to "Polarity" questions, the writer decided that Sister A was older, more headstrong and inclined towards security. Sister B was younger, more heartfelt and had a taste for adventure. A good start, and from it we deduced that Sister A is the alpha female who (as the story begins) can always rely on her younger beta sister to be a trusted sidekick.

The Polarities tool was generating the basics of the conflict that would drive the story.

The writer had envisioned a romantic setting of upper-class wealth and privilege. Our storytelling tools helped us infer that such privilege would be rooted in long-time traditions and rules to maintain the luxurious status quo. This suggested that alpha Sister A could be a conservative figure, devoted to following and protecting those rules. Polarities could posit beta Sister B as a potential radical who might be tempted away.

What could tempt her? What might threaten the status quo and tear the girls apart? How about the arrival of a swarthy, handsome fellow from the lower classes? Sister A could see this fellow through the eyes of traditional values and immediately pigeonhole him in a subservient position. But Sister B might see instead the fellow's natural charm and the possibility of a romantic relationship. Eureka! We were finding a story!

AN ESSENTIAL TOOL

Polar Opposition is one of the tools that all good dramatic craftspeople value. On the most fundamental level, stories pit two opposing forces against each other and then stage scenes of physical, emotional and philosophical combat (i.e., Reciprocal Action) until the conflict is resolved. The conflict usually continues until one of the Polar Opposites prevails or until the two forge something new that wasn't present in the early going.

PULP FICTION: TWO CHARACTERS, TWO POLES

Think about the post-credit opening of Quentin Tarantino's *Pulp Fiction*. We initially see Jules and Vincent as a matched pair of businessmen, colleagues who are carpooling to work. They are almost mundane as Vincent describes his recent vacation in Europe.

But Tarantino uses these two as Polarities to personify the opposing forces of his morality play. The separation begins when the two argue over whether giving a woman a foot massage is a sexual act. This lively debate creates conflict between the otherwise identical colleagues.

The Polar Opposition becomes clear during a key dramatic event. Jules and Vincent complete their mission by blowing away a roomful of bad boys. Out of nowhere, a previously unseen enemy barges into the room and opens fire with a hand cannon. Impossibly, all of the bullets miss Jules and Vincent.

In this all-important moment, Vincent claims that they were lucky. Jules rejects this, claiming that they've been saved by a miracle. The two characters are in thematic conflict, and the Polar Opposites argument focuses the script's actions. *Pulp Fiction* begs the question: Are we merely subject to random good and bad luck? Or is there a greater force at hand with which we can communicate?

Pulp Fiction implicitly debates this thematic question at all points. Is it luck or God that causes fugitive boxer Butch to encounter Marcellus on the street? Is he lucky or divinely inspired when he wins redemption by rescuing Marcellus from the evil gun shop owners? Is it fate that puts the watch from Butch's father at hazard?

Tarantino seems to have strong feelings about this question. Just look at where Vincent and Jules wind up. Placing his faith in luck, Vincent survives a near-fatal night out with Marcellus' wife. His luck runs out when gun-toting Butch catches him on the toilet. Denying God, Vincent dies as a secondary character in someone else's story.

Belief in God gives our Polar Opposite character superhuman powers. Faith allows unarmed Jules not only to talk mad killer Ringo and his wildly unstable girlfriend Honey Bunny out of hurting anyone in the diner, he also convinces the homicidal pair to return his wallet and Marcellus' mysterious suitcase.

In the thematic play Tarantino is staging, faith in the divine leads to control and mastery while belief in luck puts one at the mercy of random events.

Once we become aware of the Polar Opposites in play, we stick with the story. Suspense tightens as we root for one side or the other to prevail or to hope that the polar conflict will lead to a new possibility by the end.

The Polarities don't get much more obvious than this image from Snow White. *What do Snow White and the Queen represent?*

THE BRIDGES OF MADISON COUNTY: ONE CHARACTER, TWO POLES

Polar Opposites can occur within a single character. In Clint Eastwood's *The Bridges of Madison County*, Francesca is a loving Iowa farm wife who supports her husband and kids in their mundane pursuits. But she's also a displaced Italian with music and romance in her soul. Her inner being embodies two Polar Opposites.

Screenwriter Richard LaGravenese dramatizes the polarities when he temporarily removes Francesca's family, slightly altering her Ordinary World. LaGravenese then has globetrotting Robert bring the world and the possibility of extramarital romance to Francesca's doorstep. A good wife would shun him. A romantic Italian would woo him. Which Polar Opposite within her will respond?

By the time the film reaches its climax, the new lovers must decide how to proceed. Francesca returns to her role as farm wife, but the romantic in her will continue to live, too.

She becomes something that she wasn't before. The same is true of gadfly Robert. Until meeting Francesca, he was taking each moment on its own terms. As he leaves her, she has given him a spiritual home which will live in his heart for the rest of his life.

The Bridges of Madison County succeeds because its Polar Opposites are both complex and clear. The two poles are joined together to create something that hadn't existed at the beginning of the story.

The point is that the matter of Polar Opposites is a tool that opens an entire realm of productive questions that can launch the storyteller forward and can craft the inspirational visions into a workable dramatic structure.

THINGS TO THINK ABOUT

1. What are some of the Polar Opposites in vampire movies? In the *Star Wars* movies? In *Sex and the City*?

2. Brainstorm a list of twenty possible Polar Opposite pairs (e.g., Honest vs. Deceitful, Nervous vs. Calm, Flexible vs. Unyielding). Then hatch stories and conflicts that could be generated from each pairing.

3. What Polar Opposites are present in your own life? In your family? In your local community? In your state/province? In your country? Can you generate story ideas from these polarities?

NOTE FROM VOGLER

This notion of polar opposites was among the earliest storytelling principles that David and I agreed on, finding delight in movies and plays that expressed the flip sides of a human quality, like Shakespeare's study of knighthood through his contrasting characters Henry V and Falstaff. I've written a bit about story polarity in the third edition of *The Writer's Journey*, comparing it to magnetism and electricity, and trying to describe how it sometimes reverses itself temporarily, throwing characters out of their comfort zones with comic or dramatic effects.

Perhaps David and I are drawn to polarity as a storytelling device because we are polar opposites in many ways. Compared to me, he is a neat freak, and we couldn't be more different in our approaches to deadlines. His rule is "Read the script or do the assignment as soon as it comes into your hand, then relax." Mine is "Relax and put off doing the job until the last possible moment." It has made for some interesting tensions in our professional collaborations.

CHAPTER SIX

The Memo That Started It All: A Practical Guide to *The Hero with a Thousand Faces*

 VOGLER

From time to time people ask me for a copy of the original seven-page memo that was the foundation of *The Writer's Journey*. For many years I lost track of the original version and could only offer to send people the longer versions that evolved later, or point them to my book, where the memo was embedded in the first chapter, but they weren't satisfied with these solutions, apparently believing there was something almost magical about that original terse, blunt statement of my beliefs. They had to have the "legendary seven-pager" which I had called "A Practical Guide to *The Hero with a Thousand Faces*," but I was never able to lay hands on the original short version. Until now, that is.

After upheavals of home and office, and sifting through many files and boxes, I have finally come across the raw, original text of The Memo, and I offer it here to you, with the hopes it will have some of the magical effect on you that people attribute to it.

A Practical Guide to Joseph Campbell's
The Hero with a Thousand Faces
by Christopher Vogler

"There are only two or three human stories, and they go on repeating themselves as fiercely as if they had never happened before."
— Willa Cather

INTRODUCTION

In the long run, one of the most influential books of the twentieth century may turn out to be Joseph Campbell's *The Hero with a Thousand Faces*.

The book and the ideas in it are having a major impact on writing and storytelling, but above all on movie-making. Filmmakers like John Boorman, George Miller, Steven Spielberg, George Lucas, and Francis Coppola owe their successes in part to the ageless patterns that Joseph Campbell identifies in the book.

The ideas Campbell presents in this and other books are an excellent set of analytical tools.

With them you can almost always determine what's wrong with a story that's floundering; and you can find a better solution almost any story problem by examining the pattern laid out in the book.

There's nothing new in the book. The ideas in it are older that the Pyramids, older than Stonehenge, older that the earliest cave painting.

Campbell's contribution was to gather the ideas together, recognize them, articulate them, and name them. He exposes the pattern for the first time, the pattern that lies behind every story ever told.

Campbell, now 82,* is a vigorous lover of mythology and the author of many books on the subject. For many years

---

* Mr. Campbell died in 1987.

30

he has taught, written, and lectured about the myths of all cultures in all times. *The Hero with a Thousand Faces* is the clearest statement of his observations on the most persistent theme in all of oral traditions and recorded literature — the myth of the hero.

In his study of world hero myths Campbell discovered that they are all basically the same story — retold endlessly in infinite variations. He found that all storytelling, consciously or not, follows the ancient patterns of myth, and that all stories, from the crudest jokes to the highest flights of literature, can be understood in terms of the hero myth; the "monomyth" whose principles he lays out in the book.

The theme of the hero myth is universal, occurring in every culture, in every time; it is as infinitely varied as the human race itself; and yet its basic form remains the same, an incredibly tenacious set of elements that spring in endless repetition from the deepest reaches of the mind of man.

Campbell's thinking runs parallel to that of Swiss psychologist Carl Jung, who wrote of the "archetypes" — constantly repeating characters who occur in the dreams of all people and the myths of all cultures.

Jung suggested that these archetypes are reflection of aspects of the human mind — that our personalities divide themselves into these characters to play out the drama of our lives.

He noticed a strong correspondence between his patients' dream or fantasy figures and the common archetypes of mythology, and he suggested that both were coming from a deeper source, in the "collective unconscious" of the human race.

The repeating characters of the hero myth such as the young hero, the wise old man or woman, the shapeshifting woman or man, and the shadowy antagonist are identical with the archetypes of the human mind, as revealed in dreams. That's why myths, and stories constructed on the mythological model, strike us as psychologically true.

Such stories are true models of the workings of the human mind, true maps of the psyche. They are psychologically valid and realistic even when they portray fantastic, impossible, unreal events.

This accounts for the universal power of such stories. Stories built on the model of the hero myth have an appeal that can be felt by everyone, because they spring from a universal source in the collective unconscious, and because they reflect universal concerns. They deal with the child-like but universal questions: Who am I? Where did I come from? Where will I go when I die? What is good and what is evil? What must I do about it? What will tomorrow be like? Where did yesterday go? Is there anybody else out there?

The idea imbedded in mythology and identified by Campbell in *The Hero with a Thousand Faces* can be applied to understanding any human problem. They are a great key to life as well as being a major tool for dealing more effectively with a mass audience.

If you want to understand the ideas behind the hero myth, there's no substitute for actually reading Campbell's book. It's an experience that has a way of changing people. It's also a good idea to read a lot of myths, but it amounts to the same thing since Campbell is a master storyteller who delights in illustrating his points with examples from the rich storehouse of mythology.

Campbell gives a condensed version of the basic hero myth in chapter IV, "The Keys", of *The Hero with a Thousand Faces*. I've taken the liberty of amending the outline slightly, trying to reflect some of the common themes in movies, illustrated with examples from contemporary films. I'm re-telling the hero myth in my own way, and you should feel free to do the same. Every storyteller bends the myth to his or her own purpose. That's why the hero has a thousand faces.

THE HERO'S JOURNEY OUTLINE

The Hero's Journey is a pattern of narrative identified by the American scholar Joseph Campbell that appears in drama, storytelling, myth, religious ritual, and psychological development. It describes the typical adventure of the archetype known as The Hero, the person who goes out and achieves great deeds on behalf of the group, tribe, or civilization.

Its stages are:

1. The Ordinary World. The hero, uneasy, uncomfortable or unaware, is introduced sympathetically so the audience can identify with the situation or dilemma. The hero is shown against a background of environment, heredity, and personal history. Some kind of polarity in the hero's life is pulling in different directions and causing stress.

2. The Call to Adventure. Something shakes up the situation, either from external pressures or from something rising up from deep within, so the hero must face the beginnings of change.

3. Refusal of the Call. The hero feels the fear of the unknown and tries to turn away from the adventure, however briefly. Alternately, another character may express the uncertainty and danger ahead.

4. Meeting with the Mentor. The hero comes across a seasoned traveler of the worlds who gives him or her training, equipment, or advice that will help on the journey. Or the hero reaches within to a source of courage and wisdom.

5. Crossing the Threshold. At the end of Act One, the hero commits to leaving the Ordinary World and entering a new region or condition with unfamiliar rules and values.

6. Tests, Allies and Enemies. The hero is tested and sorts out allegiances in the Special World.

7. Approach. The hero and newfound allies prepare for the major challenge in the Special World.

8. The Ordeal. Near the middle of the story, the hero enters a central space in the Special World and confronts death or faces his or her greatest fear. Out of the moment of death comes a new life.

9. The Reward. The hero takes possession of the treasure won by facing death. There may be celebration, but there is also danger of losing the treasure again.

10. The Road Back. About three-fourths of the way through the story, the hero is driven to complete the adventure, leaving the Special World to be sure the treasure is brought home. Often a chase scene signals the urgency and danger of the mission.

11. The Resurrection. At the climax, the hero is severely tested once more on the threshold of home. He or she is purified by a last sacrifice, another moment of death and rebirth, but on a higher and more complete level. By the hero's action, the polarities that were in conflict at the beginning are finally resolved.

12. Return with the Elixir. The hero returns home or continues the journey, bearing some element of the treasure that has the power to transform the world as the hero has been transformed.

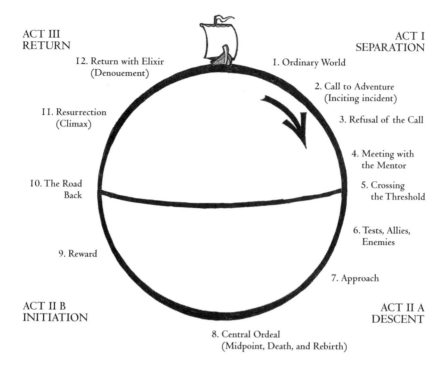

ACT III
RETURN

12. Return with Elixir
(Denouement)

11. Resurrection
(Climax)

10. The Road
Back

9. Reward

ACT II B
INITIATION

ACT I
SEPARATION

1. Ordinary World

2. Call to Adventure
(Inciting incident)

3. Refusal of the Call

4. Meeting with
the Mentor

5. Crossing
the Threshold

6. Tests, Allies,
Enemies

7. Approach

ACT II A
DESCENT

8. Central Ordeal
(Midpoint, Death, and Rebirth)

STAGES OF THE HERO'S JOURNEY

I.) The hero is introduced in his/her Ordinary World.

Most stories ultimately take us to a special world, a world that is new and alien to its hero. If you're going to tell a story about a fish out of his customary element, you first have to create a contrast by showing him in his mundane, ordinary world. In *Witness* you see both the Amish boy and the policeman in their ordinary worlds before they are thrust into alien worlds — the farm boy into the city, and the city cop into the unfamiliar countryside. In *Star Wars* you see Luke Skywalker being bored to death as a farm boy before he tackles the universe.

2.) The Call to Adventure.

The hero is presented with a problem, challenge or adventure. Maybe the land is dying, as in the King Arthur stories about the search for the Grail. In *Star Wars*, it's Princess Leia's holographic message to Obi Wan Kenobi, who then asks Luke to join the quest. In detective stories, it's the hero being offered a new case. In romantic comedies it could be the first sight of that special but annoying someone the hero or heroine will be pursuing/ sparring with.

3.) The hero is reluctant at first (Refusal of the Call).

Often at this point the hero balks at the threshold of adventure. After all, he or she is facing the greatest of all fears — fear of the unknown. At this point Luke refuses Obi Wan's call to adventure, and returns to his aunt and uncle's farmhouse, only to find they have been barbecued by the Emperor's storm troopers. Suddenly Luke is no longer reluctant, and is eager to undertake the adventure. He is motivated.

4.) The hero is encouraged by the Wise Old Man or Woman (Meeting with the Mentor).

By this time many stories will have introduced a Merlin-like character who is the hero's mentor. In *Jaws* it's the crusty Robert Shaw character who knows all about sharks; in the mythology of the *Mary Tyler Moore Show*, it's Lou Grant. The mentor gives advice and sometimes magical weapons. This is Obi Wan giving Luke his father's light saber.

The mentor can go so far with the hero. Eventually the hero must face the unknown by himself. Sometimes the Wise Old Man/Woman is required to give the hero a swift kick in the pants to get the adventure going.

5.) The hero passes the first threshold (Crossing the Threshold).

The hero fully enters the special world of the story for the first time. This is the moment at which the story takes off and the adventure gets going. The balloon goes up, the romance begins, the spaceship blasts off, the wagon train gets rolling. Dorothy sets out on the Yellow Brick Road. The hero is now committed to his/her journey and there's no turning back.

6.) The hero encounters tests and helpers (Tests, Allies, Enemies).

The hero is forced to make allies and enemies in the special world, and to pass certain tests and challenges that are part of his/her training. In *Star Wars* the cantina is the setting for the forging of an important alliance with Han Solo and the start of an important enmity with Jabba the Hutt. In *Casablanca*, Rick's Café is the setting for the "alliances and enmities" phase, and in many Westerns it's the saloon where these relationships are tested.

7.) The hero reaches the innermost cave (Approach to the Innermost Cave).

The hero comes at last to a dangerous place, often deep underground, where the object of the quest is hidden. In the Arthurian stories the Chapel Perilous is the dangerous chamber where the seeker finds the Grail. In many myths the hero has to descend into hell to retrieve a loved one, or into a cave to fight a dragon and gain a treasure. It's Theseus going to the Labyrinth to face the Minotaur. In *Star Wars* it's Luke and company being sucked into the Death Star where they will rescue Princess Leia. Sometimes it's just the hero going into his/her own dream world to confront fears and overcome them.

8.) The hero endures a central Ordeal.

This is the moment at which the hero touches bottom. He/ she faces the possibility of death, brought to the brink in a fight with a mythical beast. For us, the audience standing outside the cave waiting for the victor to emerge, it's a black moment. In *Star Wars*, it's the harrowing moment in the bowels of the Death Star, where Luke, Leia and company are trapped in the giant trash-masher. Luke is pulled under by the tentacled monster that lives in the sewage and is held down so long that the audience begins to wonder if he's dead. In *E.T., The Extraterrestrial*, E. T. momentarily appears to die on the operating table.

This is a critical moment in any story, an ordeal in which the hero appears to die and be born again. It's a major source of the magic of the hero myth. What happens is that the audience has been led to identify with the hero. We are encouraged to experience the brink-of-death feeling with the hero. We are temporarily depressed, and then we are revived by the hero's return from death.

This is the magic of any well-designed amusement park thrill ride. Space Mountain or the Great Whiteknuckler make the passengers feel like they're going to die, and there's a great thrill that comes with surviving a moment like that. This is also the trick of rites of passage and rites of initiation into fraternities and secret societies. The initiate is forced to taste death and experience resurrection. You're never more alive than when you think you're going to die.

9.) The hero seizes the sword (Seizing the Sword, Reward).

Having survived death, beaten the dragon, slain the Minotaur, the hero now takes possession of the treasure he's come seeking. Sometimes it's a special weapon like a magic sword or it may be a token like the Grail or some elixir which can heal the wounded land.

The hero may settle a conflict with his father or with his shadowy nemesis. In *Return of the Jedi*, Luke is reconciled with both, as he discovers that the dying Darth Vader is his father, and not such a bad guy after all.

The hero may also be reconciled with a woman. Often she is the treasure he's come to win or rescue, and there is often a love scene or sacred marriage at this point. Women in these stories (or men if the hero is female) tend to be shape-shifters. They appear to change in form or age, reflecting the confusing and constantly changing aspects of the opposite sex as seen from the hero's point of view. The hero's supreme ordeal may grant him a better understanding of women, leading to a reconciliation with the opposite sex.

10.) The Road Back.

The hero's not out of the woods yet. Some of the best chase scenes come at this point, as the hero is pursued by the vengeful forces from whom he has stolen the elixir or the treasure. This is the chase as Luke and friends are escaping from the Death Star, with Princess Leia and the plans that will bring down Darth Vader.

If the hero has not yet managed to reconcile with his father or the gods, they may come raging after him at this point. This is the moonlight bicycle flight of Elliott and E. T. as they escape from "Keys" (Peter Coyote), a force representing governmental authority. By the end of the movie Keys and Elliott have been reconciled and it even looks like Keys will end up as Elliott's stepfather.

11.) Resurrection.

The hero emerges from the special world, transformed by his/her experience. There is often a replay here of the mock death-and-rebirth of Stage 8, as the hero once again faces death and survives. The *Star Wars* movies play with this theme constantly — often featuring a final battle scene in which Luke is almost killed, appears to be dead for a moment, and then miraculously survives. He is transformed into a new being by his experience.

12.) Return with the Elixir

The hero comes back to the ordinary world, but the adventure would be meaningless unless he/she brought back the elixir, treasure, or some lesson from the special world. Sometimes it's just knowledge or experience, but unless he comes back with the elixir or some boon to mankind, he's doomed to repeat the adventure until he does. Many comedies use this ending, as a foolish character refuses to learn his lesson and embarks on the same folly that got him in trouble in the first place.

Sometimes the boon is treasure won on the quest, or love, or just the knowledge that the special world exists and can be survived. Sometimes it's just coming home with a good story to tell.

The hero's journey, once more: The hero is introduced in his Ordinary World where he receives the Call to Adventure. He is Reluctant at first to Cross the First Threshold where he eventually encounters Tests, Allies and Enemies. He reaches the Innermost Cave where he endures the Supreme Ordeal. He Seizes the Sword or the treasure and is pursued on the Road Back to his world. He is Resurrected and transformed by his experience. He Returns to his ordinary world with a treasure, boon, or Elixir to benefit his world.

As with any formula, there are pitfalls to be avoided. Following the guidelines of myth too rigidly can lead to a stiff, unnatural structure, and there is the danger of being too obvious. The hero myth is a skeleton that should be masked with the details of the individual story, and the structure should not call attention to itself. The order of the hero's stages as given here is only one of many variations — the stages can be deleted, added to, and drastically re-shuffled without losing any of their power.

The values of the myth are what matters. The images of the basic version — young heroes seeking magic swords from old wizards, fighting evil dragons in deep caves, etc. — are just symbols and can be changed infinitely to suit the story at hand.

The myth is easily translated to contemporary dramas, comedies, romances, or action-adventures by substituting modern equivalents for the symbolic figures and props of the hero story. The Wise Old Man may be a real shaman or wizard, but he can also be any kind of mentor or teacher, doctor or therapist, crusty but benign boss, tough but fair top sergeant, parent, grandfather, etc. Modern heroes may not be going into caves and labyrinths to fight their mythical beasts, but they do enter an innermost cave by going into space, to the bottom of the sea, into their own minds, or into the depths of a modern city.

The myth can be used to tell the simplest comic book story or the most sophisticated drama. It grows and matures as new experiments are tried within its basic framework. Changing the sex and ages of the basic characters only makes it more interesting and allows for ever more complex webs of understanding to be spun among them. The essential characters can be combined or divided into several figures to show different aspects of the same idea. The myth is infinitely flexible, capable of endless variation without sacrificing any of its magic, and it will outlive us all.

NOTE FROM McKENNA

This memo has been chewed over by more insightful people than me for nearly twenty years. Its significance has been time-tested, so I won't gild the lily. But I want to note here that I am proud of my friend for distilling it and proud of my small role in coaxing it to fruition.

I've used it for a very long time as the basis of a three-hour lecture I deliver. The idea of sitting and listening for that long a time is appalling, but something magical happens whenever people hear it.

I've heard grunts and giggles from audience members when they encounter something within the lecture that they've always known but have forgotten. I've had creatively blocked writers tell me afterwards that the lecture tapped new wellsprings of imagination for them.

My mother (who has absolutely no artistic ambitions or intentions) has attended the lecture at least a dozen times. At first, she was simply overjoyed to watch her son in teaching action. But she's returned as often as she has because the lecture makes her realize how smart she is. She's been a lifelong movie fan, and the steps of the Hero's Journey cause her to remember how deeply she appreciates films and to remind herself that she's a hero on a journey of her own.

On the following pages we reproduce the images from *The Writer's Journey 3rd Edition* illustrating the stages of the Journey. These drawings by Michele Montez and Fritz Springmeyer are beautiful objects to contemplate and may illuminate more possibilities in the stages of the Hero's Journey.

THE STAGES OF THE JOURNEY

THE ORDINARY WORLD

THE CALL TO ADVENTURE

REFUSAL OF THE CALL

MEETING WITH THE MENTOR

CROSSING THE THRESHOLD

TESTS, ALLIES, ENEMIES

APPROACH TO THE INNERMOST CAVE

THE ORDEAL

SEIZING THE SWORD, REWARD

THE ROAD BACK

RESURRECTION

RETURN WITH THE ELIXIR

CHAPTER SEVEN

The Hero's Inner Journey

VOGLER

In the course of working on adaptations of classic fairy tales at Disney animation, I came to a conclusion, that in a good tale there are two stories being told: an outward journey that puts the hero in physical danger while trying to achieving some external goal, and an inward journey that tests the hero in the arena of emotions and character, where the hero must learn some lesson or develop some missing aspect of personality. Every story needs an outer and an inner problem for the hero to solve. Every story needs to pose an outer and an inner question. The outer question: Will the hero achieve his or her external goal? Will Dorothy find her way back home from Oz? Will Frodo deliver the Ring to Mount Doom, defeating Sauron? The inner question: Will the hero learn his or her lesson in life, becoming more human, more responsible, more conscious or more complete? Will Dorothy and her companions learn self-confidence and that "There's no place like home"? Will Frodo overcome the temptations of power?

Further, I concluded the two levels of the story work together. The outward journey is usually driven by something the hero wants or desires. The story "hears" the hero's wish and provides a complex series of obstacles to achieving that goal. Along the way, the story teaches the hero a series of lessons that cause him or her to realize that something else was missing, something the hero deeply needs on a personal, emotional or psychological level. The hero, at first unaware of a personal problem or lack, slowly becomes conscious and makes changes to get what he or she really needs. The story may grant the hero's original wish and the hero may get exactly what he or she wanted, but the higher purpose of the story has also been served, leading the hero on an inward journey of self-knowledge.

With this dual journey in mind, here is another version of the Hero's Journey cycle, this time focusing on the step-by-step changes in consciousness that a typical hero might encounter on the inward journey.

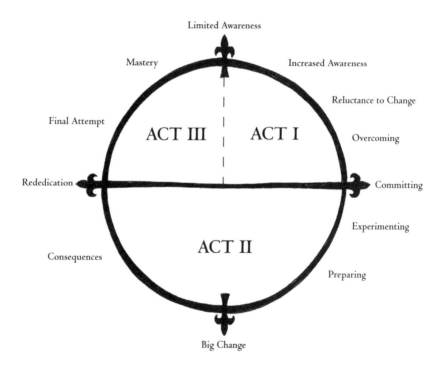

Much has been written in screenwriting manuals and studio notes about the "character arc," the imaginary trajectory of a character's development, in which he or she changes by small, believable increments, experimenting with change, threatening to fall back into old patterns, but ultimately learning life lessons and perhaps making emotional breakthroughs. The Inner

Journey is one way of describing a general pattern of character development, specifically noting how any character deals with change.

The hero's Inner Journey could be described as follows:

1. At first the hero, living in the Ordinary World, has Limited Awareness of a problem, and has been getting along using strategies that no longer work very well.

2. With Increased Awareness the hero, through a Call to Adventure, begins to realize change is urgently needed but still doesn't know what to do about it.

3. Fear and Resistance to Change are the natural reactions to facing the unknown; the hero may be momentarily paralyzed or in denial. Good intentions may be undermined by doubt (Refusal of the Call).

4. The hero seeks out a source of wisdom and inner strength, Overcoming Fear (equivalent to Meeting with the Mentor).

5. Encouraged or forced by circumstances, the hero crosses an inner Threshold by Committing to Change.

6. Now in a deeper place the hero learns the ropes of an inner Special World, Experimenting with New Conditions, testing his powers and learning who are his inner Allies and Enemies.

7. During the outer journey stage of Approach, the hero is inwardly Preparing for Major Change by exploring feelings more deeply and building up resolve to face something difficult and scary.

8. The outer Ordeal is accompanied by an inward Big Change with the Feeling of Life and Death. An old idea of the self dies under extreme pressure. Illusions are shattered, but from the tumult and destruction a new concept of the self is born.

9. While claiming some outer Reward the hero is inwardly Accepting Consequences of New Life, perhaps enjoying a feeling of love or connectedness, or realizing the consequences of the inner change he has just made.

10. On the physical Road Back, the hero inevitably is tested on the inner plane with a New Challenge requiring Re-Dedication. Physical chases, escapes and rescues may mirror inner temptations and backsliding into old patterns of behavior, or there may be new, unexpected challenges to the hero's intention to change. The world may refuse to accept the hero's new status and try to drive him back to his old condition.

11. The physical transformation or Resurrection of the hero is the outward expression of the hero's Lasting Commitment to Change but there may be Last Minute Dangers waiting to turn the inner story into a tragedy.

12. The hero usually overcomes the physical problems and makes progress on the emotional ones, achieving Mastery or experiencing a Sacred Marriage, in which warring opposite sides of a personality are brought into harmony and balance.

This is only a modest beginning at charting the Hero's Inner Journey. Good work in this area has been done by my colleague Michael Hauge with whom I did a DVD called *The Hero's Two Journeys*. Michael has deep psychological insight into how this inner journey plays out in movies, and an entertaining, easily understood way of talking about it. He reveals how characters learn to compare their inner idea of themselves with reality, and how they make the changes necessary to achieve inner peace.

Another path to understanding the possibilities of the inner journey is Jungian psychology, particularly the concept of individuation. According to this analysis of human psychological development, each of us is constantly flowing back and forth between the need to experience individual identity and the need to feel part of something, through the connection to another person, a family, a tribe, or some such grouping of society. In childhood and youth we struggle to separate ourselves from our mothers and our families while we try to individualize our personalities. In later life the task may be to integrate our personalities with people and groups, only to seek individual identity once more, until we are finally absorbed again by the mystery from which we came. The stages of individuation match well with the way-stations of the Hero's Journey, especially the inner journey, and Joseph Campbell's work suggests that the journeys of mythic heroes can be read as maps of the individuation process in story form.

PLOT-DRIVEN OR CHARACTER-DRIVEN?

But which should dominate in a story, the inner or outer dimension? That depends on the story. In Hollywood language, movies are either plot-driven (dominated by the external, action plot) or character-driven (dominated by the inner life of the characters), but in fact every movie is driven by a bit of both. In a plot-driven movie like *Avatar* the outer action plot dominates but there is still a romance and a bit of an inner character problem for the hero to solve — will he ever take something seriously and earn the respect of the Na'vi? In a character-driven movie like *Crazy Heart* the filmmakers are mainly interested in emotion and in giving us a detailed portrait of a unique character, but there is enough action plot (a car crash and a missing boy) and enough of an external goal (getting back into the song-writing game) to ground it in the world of physical consequences.

The best movies manage to satisfy us on both levels, giving us a physical journey balanced by an emotional voyage, and problems to be worked out in both dimensions. Every hero is driven by inner and outer wants and desires, faces inner and outer obstacles, and should go through internal and external transformation. You may start writing with an outward journey, but sooner or later you'll need to flesh it out with an equally compelling inner quest. What really gives stories depth, meaning, and emotional resonance is the journey of the heart and spirit and the lessons characters learn about life.

Remember always that the needs of your story dictate the structure of your story. These psychological or emotional stages could be represented by separate scenes, standing apart from the action scenes that advance the outward journey. Or they could be seamlessly woven into the plot, inseparable from the action scenes, with the emotional realizations coming in lockstep with the external trials and deeds of your hero. Either way, don't forget to develop the inner journeys, for it is these that the audience members really crave, to seek insight into themselves by comparing their lives to those of the heroes.

NOTE FROM McKENNA

I firmly believe that the stories that move us most are those that satisfy on both the "inner" and "outer" levels.

Many projects concentrate on one or the other. Arguably the old James Bond flicks are all "outer": boys-with-toys thrill rides devoted to whiz-bang set pieces and product placements. No wonder that Sean Connery (aka The Greatest Bond Ever) wearied of playing the role.

To some extent, daytime TV serials are "inner"-driven in which characters mull their emotional landscapes and writers hatch extreme inventions to fuel the slow-motion plot. (Mario Vargas Llosa's brilliant novel *Aunt Julia and the Scriptwriter* depicts a soap opera genius who is driven to madness when he's forced to create a daily dozen hours of soap opera programming.)

Ya gotta have both if your story is going to last.

Rocky is a great boxing movie and *Star Wars* created a new high water mark for sci-fi action. But they remain relevant decades later only because the lead heroes come of inner emotional age during them. The James Bond movies (and their commercial twins, based on Jason Bourne) re-boot by giving their Peter Pan heroes inner lives as fiery as their outward feats of derring-do. Prison movies and horror movies come and go. *The Shawshank Redemption* and *The Silence of the Lambs* stand above the rest because they are (among other things) deftly telling unusual love stories.

My fan loyalty is fierce, but it's reserved for movies that both goggle my eyes and touch my heart.

CHAPTER EIGHT

Reciprocal Action

—— McKENNA ——

The primary building block of all drama is Reciprocal Action. It is the substance that makes drama so compelling to an audience.

That's a bold statement. What is Reciprocal Action and how does it work?

We'll get going with another bold statement: Character doesn't exist until someone has a "want" and takes an action to have that "want" fulfilled. Here's where the fun begins...

In drama, the "wanting" character (let's call him "A") approaches another ("B") and takes action to achieve his objective. The second character, "B," has a "want" too, that usually conflicts with A's "want." Approached by A, B sees an opportunity to fulfill his objective. He adjusts and sends an action back to A.

A's approach (expressed as an active verb) and B's response (also expressed by an active verb) begin a negotiation, a combat, a game of Reciprocal Action that continues and expands until either

- ❖ A gets what he wants,
- ❖ B gets what he wants,
- ❖ some compromise is achieved or
- ❖ an external event causes an interruption.

In my experience, these are the only four outcomes possible.

OK, that's so arid a thought that even I don't get it. Let's think about it this way:

IT'S ALL A GAME

Dramatic scenes are a tennis game. Venus Williams ("A") faces off against her sister Serena ("B") in the finals of a big tournament. Both are characters because they have "wants" (each sister wants to win the current point) and are making choices and adjustments in response to the obstacle the other presents.

So Venus blasts a serve towards Serena. Venus will be very happy if her serve "aces" and quickly wins her the point. But a good dramatic scene strives for lively play and keeps the payoff in doubt for as long as possible.

So in the tennis drama we are building, Venus fires off her serve, but Serena sees it, adjusts and responds with a Reciprocal Action. Serena may fire off a rocket return shot. Having failed to "ace," Venus adjusts and hits a lob back to Serena.

More adjustment. Serena recognizes that the return is slower than what she'd expected. She moves in, waits for the ball to arrive and taps it to Venus's weak side. Venus adjusts and responds with another return. Serena adjusts and responds again. So does Venus. Each is probing for vulnerability in the opponent in order to win the point.

This continues until we achieve the outcome. Venus wins the point. Or Serena wins the point. Or they both decide to call it quits in the middle of the volley. Or a sudden thunderstorm interrupts the game.

Although the weapons in drama may not be tennis equipment, the analogy still holds.

Ilsa wants the letters of transit and has a gun to back up her "want." What does Rick want? The script for Casablanca *works because the writing team expresses subtextual themes of honor, integrity, responsibility, and love in terms of dramatic conflict and Reciprocal Action.*

Let's use the showdown scene from *Casablanca* (end of Act Two) as an example. Ilsa desperately needs the letters of transit Rick holds. This is her "want," and she corners Rick in his apartment to get them. But Rick has a "want" too, and the Reciprocal Action he takes with Ilsa eventually reveals what it is.

Ilsa opens her quest by referring to Rick as "Richard," the name she used when they were lovers in Paris. Rick sees what she's after, adjusts and shoots this gambit down. Having failed to "ace," Ilsa adjusts. She will cope with him as a businessman, inviting him to name any price. But nothing material will fulfill Rick's "want." "It's no deal."

What new tactic can Ilsa bring to bear? Perhaps she can rekindle Rick's latent idealism. She reminds him that she, Rick, and Laszlo are fighting for the same noble cause. Rick adjusts and deflects her, claiming that he is no longer involved in causes. Maybe she can re-open his heart by referring to the lovers they once were. He mocks this as a cynical ploy: too little, too late to be believed.

Ilsa adjusts again. She insults Rick, calling him a coward. Rick knows how weak this weapon is. He adjusts and stares her down, causing her to retreat. Another adjustment as Ilsa pleads for the very life of the world. He adjusts and blasts her with cold indifference: "What of it? I'm going to die in Casablanca. It's a good spot for it."

Out of options, Ilsa makes her final reciprocal attack. She pulls a pistol. If Rick is so willing to die, she will give him death to get she wants. Seeing the gun, Rick again adjusts and challenges her by walking into her line of fire: "Go ahead and shoot. You'll be doing me a favor."

Does she pull the trigger? Of course not: this is one of Hollywood's great love stories. Instead, she gives Rick what he has wanted all along: acknowledgment that she has always loved him and still does. Rick wins the point in a very satisfying game of Reciprocal Action.

Almost all effective dramatic writing is based in this form of reciprocity.

In the opening scene of *The Godfather*, Sicilian-American Bonasera wants Don Corleone to avenge the outrage that has been inflicted on his innocent daughter. Such vengeance is easily within the Don's power, but he demurs when Bonasera offers money and favor: "I'll give you anything you want, but do what I ask."

What does the Don want? One word for it is "respect," and until Bonasera voluntarily kisses the Don's ring and embraces him as his "Godfather," the request is denied. Take a look at that scene to see how the two reciprocal actors play against each other until the victor causes the vanquished to submit.

For that matter, take a look at any scene in almost any screenplay and see how the play gets played in terms of Reciprocal Action.

Reciprocal Action is how dramatists give us information. Essayists can expound philosophically about their themes. News writers relay facts of an event to us directly. Novelists can allow their characters to speak to us directly about their impressions and private thoughts.

But it's the way of the dramatist to place opposing characters at war with each other so that we can see the forces in action and determine for ourselves the nature of each as the combat continues.

Reciprocal Action is essential to dramatic storytelling and the way that good dramatists seduce us into the worlds they are creating.

THINGS TO THINK ABOUT

1. Lift a dialogue scene from an existing script. Assign a verb to each line of dialogue to specify what the active character is doing to the receiver. You are looking for the subtext, so don't trap yourself by thinking only of what the text says (e.g., people frequently say one thing and mean another). The more active the verb, the better (e.g., "prods" or "seduces" is more effective than "questions" or "claims"). Don't settle for the obvious. Figure out what the active character wants and what tactic each line of dialogue is using to achieve that objective.

2. Imagine an active image (e.g., a fistfight, a footrace). Use this active image as the subtext for a dialogue scene in which two characters use language to achieve their objectives.

NOTE FROM VOGLER

David is much more of a sportsman than I, as you can see from his frequent use of sports analogies. Sports and games are his mythology, and one way in which he dominates me in the subtle competition that is part of any long friendship. So he may have a better intuitive grasp of this Reciprocal Action concept than I. Although, come to think of it, I was pretty good at fencing in college and so I understand how blows and counter-blows are exchanged, how you feint, parry and thrust until a fatal blow is landed. David still shudders when he remembers how we once went out into the back yard with wooden practice swords. He seemed to be beating me at my own game with his quick parries and fancy footwork, but I pulled off a surprising spin-turn that would have cut his legs off if we'd been using live blades. There's Reciprocal Action for you.

CHAPTER NINE

OUT OF CHARACTER: THE ARCHETYPES AND OTHER WAYS TO LOOK AT CHARACTER

——— VOGLER ———

THE ARCHETYPES

Archetypes are recurring patterns of human behavior, symbolized by standard types of characters in movies and stories. Here is a brief checklist of the common archetypes. More detailed descriptions can be found in *The Writer's Journey*.

HEROES

Central figures in stories. Everyone is the hero of his or her own myth. The hero is usually the character who has the most to learn, and the longest journey to make. The classical ideal of the hero was one willing to sacrifice personal desires on behalf of something greater.

SHADOWS

Villains and enemies, perhaps the enemy within. The dark side of the Force, the repressed possibilities of the hero, his or her potential for evil. Can be other kinds of repression, such as repressed grief, anger, frustration or creativity that is dangerous if it doesn't have an outlet. Some stories have no formal villain or antagonist character, but the hero still has to overcome some lack, absence, obstacle or force of nature that is a Shadow to him.

MENTORS

The hero's guide or guiding principles. Yoda, Merlin, a great coach or teacher. Could also be an instinct, an inner code of behavior.

HERALDS

Those who bring the Call to Adventure. Could be persons or events that call the hero to action. The job of bringing the Call may be a function performed briefly by a Mentor, a Shapeshifter or even, on occasion, a Shadow. Or a new character can be created to do only this task.

THRESHOLD GUARDIANS

The forces that stand in the hero's way at important turning points, including jealous enemies, professional gatekeepers, or the hero's own fears and doubts. Myths are filled with examples of ways that heroes outwit, hoodwink, get around, seduce, trick, mimic, undermine, climb over, recruit or bedazzle these guardians of the boundaries between worlds.

SHAPESHIFTERS

In horror and fantasy stories, creatures like vampires or werewolves who change shape. Shapeshifters are symbolic representations of the way even our own personalities and moods are subject to baffling change. In dealing with others in the arenas of love, friendship, and teamwork, the hero often experiences the other characters as alarmingly changeable or two-faced. "Appearances can be deceiving" is a lesson stories keep teaching us. To Luke Skywalker, Obi Wan Kenobi appears at first as an eccentric but unimportant hermit, but then reveals himself as a Jedi master with great power and influence. Princess Leia is mercurial in Luke's eyes, imperious and haughty one moment, tender or flirtatious in the next. Han

Solo comes on as a cocky and selfish space cowboy whose loyalty is uncertain, but eventually transforms into a hero capable of self-sacrifice. Luke experiences all the characters through a first impression that gives way to another reality. Even Darth Vader reveals another dimension behind his mask, a secret identity as Luke's father, once a young idealist like him.

Heroes too can wear the cloak and mask of the Shapeshifter. They are often required to disguise themselves to get past a Threshold Guardian and may take on the form of other people or creatures in order to "get into their skin" or walk in their shoes, so as to understand what they go through. *Tootsie* forces a male actor to assume a female role and gives him a deep understanding of the feminine.

In romance, the loved one may appear changeable, inconstant, saying one thing and meaning another. Because the motif is so consistent in the romantic subplots of movies, I have placed the hero's "love interest" (old Hollywood term for the person the hero is romantically involved with) under the heading of the Shapeshifter. The hero may look at the loved or desired one as a Mentor or Ally at times, perhaps even as a Shadow occasionally, but primarily they seem to experience the lover as a Shapeshifter.

I also find the Shapeshifter idea useful for describing what happens in "two-handers" or buddy comedies where the main emotional bond is not a romantic or sexual one, but a bond of friendship or partnership. Two people with contrasting traits are thrown together to achieve a common goal, with comic or dramatic results from the collision of their personal styles and philosophies. In most cases, the audience will tend to identify with one of the two, perhaps the narrator or the more "normal" of the two. From the point of view of that "audience character," the other member of the team will be experienced as a Shapeshifter, whose loyalty is in question and who keeps surprising the first character with new revelations about his true nature.

TRICKSTERS

Clowns and mischief-makers such as Bugs Bunny, Daffy Duck, Richard Pryor and Eddie Murphy. Our own mischievous subconscious, urging us to change. Tricksters reverse the normal conditions of society to expose its flaws. The Trickster can be a secondary character but is capable of carrying a story as a Trickster Hero. Europe's medieval jester, Till Eulenspiegel, subject of an animated feature I wrote for a German production, is the irreverent hero of a huge cycle of tales.

ALLIES

Characters who help the hero through the change. Sidekicks, buddies, girlfriends who advise the hero through the transitions of life. They are expendable and can be injured, kidnapped, or killed to motivate the hero and create sympathy.

PROPP'S CHARACTERS

An interesting and revealing variant on the archetypes can be found in the work of Russian scholar Vladimir Propp on a sampling of 103 Russian fairy tales. (See chapters 13 and 14 on Propp's 31 Story Functions and his notion of character.) He identifies the following character types.

I. The villain — struggles against the hero. Can seek or get information, make plans to deceive the hero, trick the hero into helping the villain, harm others (kill, kidnap, torture, enslave, enchant, vampirize, turn into zombies, etc.). Can be defeated, taunt, pursue, seek revenge, make false claim, compete with hero in impossible tests, be found out, get his punishment. Equivalent to the hero's journey Shadow or antagonist. (Note that in some stories Propp found a second villain, the false claimant who appears near the end of the story, after the first villain has been killed or defeated.)

2. The donor — prepares the hero or gives the hero some magical object. (Equivalent to the Mentor. May be combined with #3 and/or #5.)

3. The (magical) helper — helps the hero in the quest. Magical animals, objects like flying carpets and powers like invisibility operate just as human helpers do and follow the same rules. (Equivalent to the hero's Ally.)

4. The princess and her father — the princess may become the object of the quest when she has been kidnapped or imprisoned. Otherwise, Propp says the princess and her father are interchangeable as to their function in the tale, though obviously, the princess can marry the hero and the king can grant him all or part of his kingdom. The essence is a love interest or an authority figure who assigns a difficult task to the hero, identifies and punishes the false hero, and rewards the hero. Princess Leia in *Star Wars* follows this fairy tale format, by being taken prisoner by the forces of darkness, being rescued by the hero and then rewarding him in a ceremonial way at the end.

   This set of functions can be related to the Shapeshifter archetype because the characters may change their orientation towards the hero at different moments in the plot, sometimes seeking the hero's help and granting him approval, while at other times doubting him and making his life more difficult.

5. The "dispatcher" — makes the Lack known and sends the hero off. This is a job which may be performed by the donor character, or a new character may be introduced solely to perform this function. (Equivalent to the Herald.)

6. The hero or victim/seeker hero — leaves home, reacts to the donor, undertakes the quest, struggles with the villain or overcomes the lack, contends with the false claimant, weds the princess/claims the throne. (Accords closely with the Hero's Journey version of the hero.)

7. False hero/false claimant/second villain — takes credit for the hero's actions or tries to marry the princess/claim the throne. Competes with the hero in a difficult task or a series of three tasks. Is usually exposed as a false claimant and punished by command of the king or princess with death, exile or appropriate humiliation. (May be equivalent to the Shadow, almost an evil twin of the hero and his dark possibilities, presenting a challenge with full intensity right at the climax, at the threshold of victory. Or this figure can be seen as a kind of Threshold Guardian, providing an obstacle for the hero at the brink of victory.)

Propp calls these "characters" but they are really just the functions that different people, animals or even objects in the story can perform. Combined with the archetypes, these descriptions of essential actions in a story begin to reveal the unconscious building blocks of story and character. In order for us to recognize an account as a story, certain actions must be performed in a logical sequence, and actors with certain fundamental characteristics must be created to perform them. The archetypes and Propp's analysis of story functions provide something like an alphabet of character, a set of essential values from which a complete language of character can be built.

Of course, there are nearly infinite levels to character, and to begin to explore them, you also have to take into account human psychology, motivations, effect of social environment and a thousand other elements. David's chapters on the environmental factors that go into making characters and scenes realistic will explore some of the other possible dimensions of character. In the following chapter he will show you a powerful tool for understanding how character operates in story.

THE ARCHETYPES

THE HERO

THE MENTOR

THE THRESHOLD GUARDIAN

THE HERALD

THE SHAPESHIFTER

THE SHADOW

THE ALLY

THE TRICKSTER

CHAPTER TEN

CHARACTER:
THE ALGEBRAIC EQUATION
(AND OTHER UNNATURAL ACTS)
——— McKENNA ———

You can't tell a story without characters. But what exactly is a character? Is it the actor playing the role? Is it the make-up and costuming? Is it the dialogue being said or the physical action being taken?

To an extent the answer to all these questions is "yes." But for us writers, character is more fundamental. We create character before the casting, the costume designing and the staging of action. So how do we hatch this thing out of thin air?

I'll propose an answer that's as simple as high school algebra:

Character = Want + Motion + Obstacle + Choice

Let's break this equation down and see how it works.

WANT

As we discussed during the "Reciprocal Action" and "Want List" chapters, nothing exists in drama until somebody wants something. Without a motivating desire, "inertia of rest" keeps us in stasis, doing nothing and going nowhere. There is no reason for us to start the ball rolling until rolling the ball will lead us towards a something we "want."

That "want" can be almost anything: a beer from the fridge, freedom from religious persecution, fame and fortune, a better job, a goodnight kiss. Any of these things are capable of getting us out of our chairs, onto our feet and on the move. Drama begins (but certainly doesn't end) with "want."

Here are some examples. In *Gone, Baby, Gone*, detectives Patrick and Angie want to find little Amanda and rescue her from her kidnappers. In *Little Miss Sunshine* Olive wants to win the contest, and her besieged family joins her. In *Legally Blonde*, Elle wants to marry Warner. Each of these "wants" externalizes the character's inner state and begins to shape the drama.

MOTION

But "want" alone isn't character. Effort must be made, a motion of some kind. You can't tame the West until you saddle your horse and ride out to God's country. You can't win the title until you put on your boxing gloves and enter the arena. You can't find love if you sit at home waiting for the phone to ring.

Each of our examples activates the "want" by kicking the characters into motion. Patrick and Angie start to question people at the neighborhood bars. Olive and her family pack up their van and head towards Arizona. Elle dresses herself for her fabulous night when Warner will propose. Activated by a "want," our characters get a move on, and the stories begin.

OBSTACLE

We're getting close to Character, but there's more to this than "want" and "motion." Drama needs conflict. Our story is a long dull ride until our hero smacks into an opposing force. We need an obstacle, something between where we are and where we want to go in order to create tension, suspense, and rooting interest for the audience.

So Patrick and Angie face hard-nosed thugs in the bars who are intent on stopping them. Olive and her dysfunctional family argue amongst themselves and face disaster when the van breaks down. Warner breaks up with Elle instead of proposing to her. In each instance, an obstacle has blocked the "want." The story could end at this moment.

CHOICE

Which brings us to the last element in the equation. Once our hero wants something and moves in a direction to get it, the ball is rolling. Once an obstacle stops that ball, our hero must decide what to do about it. Does he barge straight ahead in the hope of bashing through the obstacle? Does she give up on the "want" in favor of something else? Does he make a detour, shifting to Plan B?

In short, the hero must make a "choice," and it's the specifics of that "choice" which create Character.

We discover what Patrick and Angie are all about when we see them form an alliance with the cops instead of going it alone. Their choice is specific to this story and to these characters. A writer could build an entirely different story from this situation by having heroes choose a different response to the obstacle.

Olive and her family continue to bicker, but they choose to push their obstructive van to keep the quest alive. As a family, the characters are torn apart by their individual pains, but they unite in this mutual, physicalized "choice." Writer Michael Arndt continually uses the conflict between individual pain and team effort to keep us guessing about how things will work out. Elle could easily find another fellow, but it's Warner that she wants. So she makes the extraordinary "choice" to apply for law school and to claw her way into Warner's new life at Harvard. It's not a choice most people would make, and Elle's decision to make it marks her as a very special character.

It is the Choice that Characters make that individuates them. We know who the characters are by what they choose to do. A good script constantly forces characters to make such choices in the face of their wants.

THE EQUATION AND THE UNNATURAL ACT OF SCREENWRITING

This basic character equation is the fundamental tool of dramatic storytelling. But if our stories are to sweep up our audiences we must push that fundamental to extremes.

Going to extremes in this manner makes good dramatic storytelling an unnatural act. Here's why: Like you and me, a story's hero wants instant gratification and would be happy to have his "want" satisfied on page 2.

But as storytellers who intend to get past page 2, it's up to us to keep throwing obstacles in our hero's path. Maybe the object of desire becomes inaccessible. Maybe a rival comes along to challenge us for possession of it. Maybe a second object arrives to confuse us about what we want.

Because my young screenwriting students identify with their heroes, they frequently fail to give them a dramatically hard time. But the best of my students unleash their sadistic creativity, providing one infuriating obstacle after another to force their beloved protagonists into two hours worth of "choices." These students understand the need to continually deny fulfillment to our hero in order to keep propelling the story forward.

In the old Greek myth, Orpheus wants a long and happily married life with Eurydice. But, damn it, the girl ups and dies. She's the one that he wants, so he must travel across the River Styx and into the land of the dead to get her back. Every step of the way provides more obstacles for Orpheus, and we ride along with him to see what he's willing to do to win her against these impossible odds. He is constantly facing obstacles and forced into making choices.

In *The Odyssey*, Odysseus has just finished a ten-year war in Troy and wants to get back home to the wife and kid. It's not all that far away, and a few weeks at sea should get the job done. But masterful storyteller Homer arranges for Odysseus to tick off some vengeful gods, meaning that our guy will endure shipwrecks, storms, hallucinogenic drugs, mutinous crews, man-eating monsters, and the jealous demands of at least one horny enchantress before he approaches his heart's desire. By the time he gets home, our hero has paid a heavy price. But Homer throws even more challenges at his hero on the home front to dramatize how dear Odysseus' prize truly is.

When we sadistic creators load up a character with a "want" and then place enormous obstacles between that character and the object of desire, we do the very thing that we wish to avoid in our real lives. We make it as hard as possible for our heroes to get what they want. We demand that they put their butts on the line and show us what they are made of.

It's a nasty, unnatural business, but somebody has to do it.

BTW, if you think that my references to Orpheus and Odysseus are just too creaky and old to take seriously, you might want to check out films like Baz Luhrmann's *Moulin Rouge* (a clear re-mix of elements from the former) and the Coen Brothers' *O Brother, Where Art Thou?* (a screwball comedy that re-casts Odysseus as a Mississippi convict) to see that these creaky old stories still pack plenty of kick.

THINGS TO THINK ABOUT

1. You'll only get the full benefit from the tools by putting them to work on something. Apply the Character = Want + Motion + Obstacle + Choice equation to a *Harry Potter* adventure. What does each situation and choice tell us about Harry and his classmates? How do they work for episodes of sitcoms like *Seinfeld* or in story lines from daytime dramas like *As the World Turns?*

2. Turn the Character Equation on one of your own stories. Identify the Want, Motion, Obstacle, and Choice. Can you dramatize your character's inner wants more effectively by sadistically placing Obstacles in the way?

NOTE FROM VOGLER

David, you're making me nervous with your classical references here. I'm the one who's supposed to deal out the "creaky old" mythic examples. But I have to admit Orpheus and *The Odyssey* are pretty good illustrations of your point. Now I feel tempted to compete by giving a few sports analogies, but I will resist the impulse.

This Character Equation really helped me to understand how stories work, at both the macro and micro levels. It's an accurate description of the overall arc of a story but also of the dynamics of a scene. You can look at the Equation as a series of loops: When Want, Movement, and Obstacle have led to a Choice, that Choice may generate further Wants, Obstacles, Movements, and Choices. By David's principle of Reciprocal Action, a hero's choice always has consequences and until the villains are finally defeated, they will come back with challenges to what the hero wants.

CHAPTER ELEVEN

THEOPHRASTUS, WHAT A CHARACTER!

—— VOGLER ——

"Nothing with gods, nothing with fate, Weighty affairs will just have to wait."

> — "Comedy Tonight" by Stephen Sondheim, from *A Funny Thing Happened on the Way to the Forum*

Trivia quiz: Can you name a hit Broadway musical inspired by a pamphlet written twenty-three hundred years ago — by a Lesbian? (A guy from the island of Lesbos, that is.)

Answer: The comedy classic *A Funny Thing Happened on the Way to the Forum.*

With music and lyrics by Stephen Sondheim and book by Bert Shevelove and Larry Gelbart, this long-running musical became a popular movie and is always being revived in a theatre somewhere, simply because it's so much fun, for audience and performers alike. And its roots are in a collection of comical character sketches written in the third century BCE.

The pamphlet was the work of Aristotle's star pupil, a man named Theophrastus. The trail of thought that led to *Forum* begins with his short book of character sketches, called simply *The Characters.* If we want to understand how storytellers have developed strategies for creating and describing realistic characters, we have to begin with Theophrastus. A real pioneer of character writing, he was first to attack the problem by identifying thirty familiar types of behavior he'd observed in the Athenian marketplace.

He crafted witty, economical word pictures of the survival strategies and abrasive personalities of his fellow citizens. They're still amusing to read today and the human failings they describe can be seen in any market or street in the world. With its tone of amusement at the selfish, crude, vain, and stupid tendencies of human beings, *The Characters* launched a thousand comedies upon a million stages. It still has the power to do that today and is a useful starting point for storytellers who want to breathe life into their characters.

In this chapter we will briefly note the thirty character types of Theophrastus and suggest how they might be used to create better characters. If you're really into this, do what I did when I was learning my trade. Dig up a complete text of *The Characters* and read through the sketches with an open mind. Try to find an edition illustrated with caricatures — it's fun to see how later artists tried to put comical faces to Theophrastus' gallery of human foibles. For your convenience we have summarized the thirty types so you can begin to experiment with them.

SO WHO IS THIS CHARACTER THEOPHRASTUS?

Theophrastus may not be as famous as his teacher Aristotle, but he was the next link in a remarkable chain of students and teachers that began with Socrates. Socrates taught Plato, Plato taught Aristotle, and Aristotle passed all their knowledge on to his student Theophrastus, a worthy successor.

"Theophrastus" was a nickname; his real name was Tyrtamus of Eresus, a town on the island of Lesbos. He was drawn to Athens by the beacon of knowledge that was Plato's Academy. Plato dubbed him "Theophrastus" (divine speaker), so he must have had the gift of gab. After Plato's death he became Aristotle's most loyal and hard-working student.

When Aristotle died he willed the leadership of the Academy and his entire body of knowledge to Theophrastus, who tried to live up to his teacher's high standards, producing hundreds of books on a wide variety of subjects.

Most are lost or forgotten, but fortunately for us *The Characters* survived and took on a life of its own. Rediscovered along with Aristotle's works in the Renaissance, it was widely imitated and spawned a literary genre of character sketching, a theory of personality, and a host of plays and novels drawn from its character types.

THE PLAN OF *THE CHARACTERS*

Theophrastus had a simple but revolutionary plan. He went out into the Athenian agora or marketplace and opened his eyes and listened. What he saw and heard was an amazing display of vigorous life as wily merchants jostled with stern soldiers, proud athletes and serene philosophers. He began to see patterns in the multitude, certain kinds of behavior and attitude repeated in a number of individuals until they emerged as types, categories that almost everyone could recognize. Many people seemed to share similar outlooks on life and employed similar strategies for survival and success, and thus could be recognized as types. Theophrastus simply described the predictable behavior of these categories in various social situations, spending no more than a couple of hundred words on each one.

His examples are funny and concrete. For example, among the tendencies that define the Boor is that he is likely to sit down in public in a short tunic, exposing his private parts to view. Not so different from modern plumbers bending over in droopy pants or guys at the beach in ill-considered Speedos. His tone is one of amused tolerance for the annoying habits of his fellow Athenians.

You might think behavior has evolved in twenty-three centuries, but you'd recognize most of these types in your neighborhood market or coffee shop. In most cases the name of the character type alone tells you what you need to know, but we have provided a short phrase or two to further identify each type or character trait. This is just a synopsis; there is no substitute for the droll experience of actually reading a good translation of Theophrastus.

THE CHARACTERS OF THEOPHRASTUS

- ❖ The Ironical Man is Mr. Insincerity. He's two-faced and never says what he means.

- ❖ The Flatterer butters up his betters.

- ❖ The Garrulous Man loves to hear himself talk about the most banal things.

- ❖ The Boor is loud and has no sense of good taste or manners.

- ❖ The Complaisant Man says what people want to hear and wants everyone to like him.

- ❖ The Reckless Man has poor impulse control and charges blindly into anything. Gets himself in trouble by loose, loud talk.

- ❖ The Chatty Man won't let you get a word in edgewise.

- ❖ The Gossip never heard a rumor he didn't like and embellish.

- ❖ The Shameless Man has a lot of nerve and isn't embarrassed to cut into lines, slip into events without paying, or stick his finger in the cake frosting.

- ❖ The Penurious (Penny-pinching) Man goes to ridiculous lengths to calculate profit or loss in petty affairs.

- ❖ The Gross Man is disrespectful to women and the codes of civility.

- ❖ The Unseasonable Man has no sense of timing and is always barging in at the wrong time.

⬧ The Officious Man is an intervening busybody who butts into other people's affairs.

⬧ The Stupid Man misses the point and doesn't get the joke.

⬧ The Surly Man holds grudges and snarls like a junk-yard dog.

⬧ The Superstitious Man is easily spooked and believes all the old wives' tales.

⬧ The Grumbler complains constantly that he's not being treated fairly.

⬧ The Distrustful Man is suspicious of everyone and has a low opinion of his fellow humans.

⬧ The Offensive Man is a slob who goes around in a stained tunic with food in his beard.

⬧ The Unpleasant Man has a knack for thoughtless, disgusting, inappropriate remarks.

⬧ The Man of Petty Ambition tries to show his status by keeping up with the latest fashions and puts great importance on trivial accomplishments.

⬧ The Mean Man is a cheapskate who'd take money out of a blind beggar's hand. A lousy tipper.

⬧ The Boastful Man never stops blowing his own horn about small or imaginary accomplishments.

⬧ The Arrogant Man thinks he's above it all and better than everyone else.

⬧ The Coward slinks away from confrontations but takes credit for the victory when the battle is over.

- The Oligarch (Power-monger) is hungry for power for himself and those of his class. He wants to change the rules of society to favor himself.

- The Late Learner doesn't act his age, and clings to an early stage of development. Mr. Immaturity.

- The Evil Speaker will talk behind your back and has a bad word to say about everyone.

- The Patron of Rascals hangs out with the wrong crowd and sticks up for the worst in society.

- The Avaricious (Greedy) Man thinks only about amassing wealth and tries to gain every financial advantage.

To give the flavor of these short character sketches, here are modern paraphrases of two examples, The Unseasonable Man and the Distrustful Man.

The Unseasonable Man is the master of bad timing. He will go up to a busy person and unload all his troubles in detail. He wants to romance his sweetheart when she has a fever. He shows up to give evidence when a trial is already over. If invited to a wedding he will spoil the mood by complaining loudly about womenfolk. If you've just come back from a long journey, he will propose going for a hike. If you just sold something, he'll bring you a higher bidder when it's too late. He loves to tell long stories to those who already know them by heart. If you have to punish your slave, he brings up the time his slave hung himself after being punished. He shows up just when arguing parties have arrived at a settlement, and embroils them in disagreement all over again. When he is merry with drink and wants to dance, he will grab a partner who is totally sober.

The Distrustful Man sends a second slave to market to check on the prices paid by the first slave. He carries his cash around and stops every two hundred yards to count it. On going to bed he asks his wife if the safe is closed and the doors and windows are locked, and if she says "Yes, dear" he gets up anyway and pads around in his bare feet to check everything, and hardly gets any sleep for worrying about his money and possessions being stolen. When he sends out his clothes for cleaning, he doesn't care which cleaner does the best job, but which one has the best money-back guarantee if something goes wrong. If a neighbor wants to borrow some cups, he'll refuse or make excuses if he can, but if it's a relative or a close friend, he still weighs and measures the cups and makes the borrower sign for them. He's so sure his slaves want to run away that he makes them walk in front of him so he can keep an eye on them. If you buy some small thing from him, and promise to pay him later because you aren't carrying any cash, he'll say "No problem, if you're not busy I'll just walk with you to the bank."

The Characters was revolutionary, for no one before had ever tried to catalogue ordinary human behavior in this way. Art and literature were supposed to celebrate the highest aspiration of heroes and gods, and there were very few statues made or plays written with commonplace people as subjects. *The Characters* might be the beginning of what we call social realism in the arts.

HOW TO USE *THE CHARACTERS*

When I first encountered *The Characters* it was a gift from the gods, because I had been looking for systems to deal with things like structure and character. Campbell's body of work on the Hero's Journey and Syd Field's three-act paradigm had filled in most of the blanks about structure, and Jungian archetypes had provided some tools for dealing with character, but they only got me so far. The archetypes told me something about the mythic essence of characters, but I hadn't yet figured out how to mix them up, put them into interesting contradictions, or make them seem realistic. When I needed them, *The Characters* came along to shake up my thinking and round out my set of tools.

A MENU OF POSSIBILITIES

The title of *The Characters* is a bit misleading. The sketches are not really characters in the modern sense of three-dimensional human beings with complex drives and many layers of behavior. They are, rather, a menu of possible character behaviors or character flaws. They describe some negative traits of character rather than fully fleshed-out characters with all the depth and dimension we expect. A more accurate title would have been "Aspects of Character," "Faces of Character," or something like that.

But the sketches are a starting point. You could certainly put them up on stage unadorned and get some laughs. That's exactly what Athenian playwrights did the moment the ink was dry on copies of *The Characters*. But storytellers soon learned to play the character traits like notes of music and combine them into chords. Theophrastus' slashing word portraits of his contemporaries played unvarnished on stages for centuries, but for over two thousand years they have also been used in subtle combinations to give shading and complexity to characters we love to laugh at.

MIX AND MATCH

If you just combine two or more of these characteristics, you start getting something we would recognize as a real character rather than a one-dimensional stereotype. By slapping together the Coward and the Boastful Man, for example, you can build a more realistic portrait of someone who covers for his fears and insecurities by bragging loudly, like Shakespeare's lovable rogue Falstaff. The Commedia dell'Arte's stock character Il Capitano, "The Captain," is made up of these two traits, and as more traits were added later, he became more realistic, developing into Scaramuccia or Scaramouche ("Skirmish"), a boastful coward who is also clever and a good lover, and is sometimes even capable of showing courage.

TWO IS GOOD, THREE IS BETTER

A good rule of thumb is to try to get all your characters to operate in at least three dimensions. You can look at a persona like that of the radio and TV comic Jack Benny as a combination of the Penurious Man, the Coward, and the Late Learner, because his character was cheap, fearful, and refused to accept his real age, forever insisting he was thirty-nine years old. Benny could get laughs by putting just two of these traits into conflict. The fact that he's a physical Coward comes into conflict with the Penurious, penny-pinching trait in his most famous stage bit, when a bandit holds him at gunpoint and says "Your money or your life!" and Benny replies, after a long, perfectly timed pause, "I'm thinking it over!" Benny could have built a career solely on being the Coward who is tight with money, but he was able to create many more comedy situations by adding a third quality to his stage personality, the vanity that makes him cling to his youth.

Try the experiment: Randomly pick three of the traits described by Theophrastus and create a character who displays all three of those characteristics. Try to find the connections among the traits, how one might cause the other, how they might put the character into difficult comic or dramatic situations as he or she tries to honor more than one side of his or her character at a time.

THE MORE THE MERRIER

Don't stop with combining three Theophrastean characteristics. (Try saying that three times fast.) Pile them on. See what happens if you make up a character that has ten of these behaviors. In a typical episode of *The Office*, Steve Carrel's character, the bumbling, petty boss Michael Scott, seems to display every one of the human failings in *The Characters*.

MAKE YOUR OWN LIST

Don't limit yourself to the traits observed by Theophrastus. *The Characters* should be for the storyteller the beginning of a long, long list of character traits that become part of your inventory. If you just read over the titles, you'll probably start thinking of other characteristics or familiar types that could be added to your list — The Shy Person, the Rebel, the Nerd, the Rescuer, the Blamer, the Cell Phone Addict, the Victim, the Person Who Is Always Late for Everything. If you haven't already done this kind of exercise in your development as a writer, do it now. In a quick brainstorming session, write down thirty character traits that you see in yourself or people around you.

It's probably easiest to name negative characteristics, as Theophrastus did, but you don't have to limit yourself to flaws of character. You can also list virtues or positive traits, so that your list might include the Honest Person, the Trusting Person, the Generous Person, the Truth-Teller, etc.

TRY YOUR HAND AT CHARACTER SKETCHING

Sketching a character efficiently is a skill that every novelist or screenwriter has to master, and Theophrastus is a good teacher of that skill, defining each trait with specific examples of behavior and occasional samples of characteristic dialogue.

As an experiment, pick one of these character traits from your own list and write a more detailed description, in the style of Theophrastus, maybe a couple of hundred words. Put in the typical behavior of someone with that trait, including their characteristic dialogue. How do people of that type react in given situations? How do they enter a room, walk down the street, make deals, react to news, get things done? What is their view of the world? (For example: Everyone's out to get me, there's plenty to go around, no one can be trusted, everything will always work out for the best, etc.)

Of course, this will be a generalized portrait of a type, a category of behavior. Another kind of character sketch is drawn from life, and writers need to practice this kind of sketching as well, but observing and recording general tendencies of behavior and developing categories is a useful step towards giving your imaginary characters the depth and complexity of real people.

FURTHER EXPERIMENTS

Make a game of it. Print out a list of the character types of Theophrastus or ones you have identified. Then cut them up into individual strips of paper and stir them together. Pick three at random and see what combinations you come up with. Try writing about a character who has all three of those traits. Then think up a story to go with that character.

You could even do this like a game of charades, as an opportunity to test your acting skills. Have each person in the group draw one of the characteristics from a hat and then act out that characteristic, letting the others try to guess what trait is being represented. For a bigger acting challenge, draw two or three traits at a time and see if you can successfully portray them at the same time.

Be playful, have some fun with these elements. They will help you when it's time to create characters to do specific jobs in your stories. You'll remember to make them multi-dimensional with a number of intersecting, perhaps conflicting characteristics rather than just one.

SUPPORTING ROLES

Combining and layering of traits is especially useful with secondary characters and even minor roles. Most writers know to give their heroes and villains more than one characteristic (Simba in *The Lion King* is curious, friendly and brave, the villain Scar is witty, debonair, ambitious and jealous), but the rest of the characters may only be given one trait, or they are too often presented as a stereotypical package, with a set of traits that belong to that cliché, and no surprising or contradictory qualities to make them real or interesting. A boring stock character like a detective or a villain's hulking bodyguard, even if he is in the story for only one scene and has no dialogue, can suddenly "pop" into three-dimensional life if we give him two or three unexpected character touches.

For example we could specify that in addition to being tough or mean as we might expect, our detective or henchman is also an opera lover and is sentimental about his mother. Actors know "There are no small parts, there are only small actors" and will bring some of these extra dimensions to the briefest appearance in a story. Many a character actor in old movies made an impression in a routine role by tilting a hat with a certain attitude or creating a unique walk that revealed other aspects of the character's personality.

CORRECTING THE NEGATIVE SLANT OF
THE CHARACTERS

You've probably noticed that all of the behaviors described by Theophrastus are negative traits or vices, what we might call character flaws. The negativity of *The Characters* has led some commentators to wonder if he might also have written or intended to write a balancing set of positive character types, sketching a menu of virtuous possibilities as well as moral pitfalls. In his introduction Theophrastus writes in the voice of a ninety-nine-year-old man giving advice to a friend, saying he closely observed "both the good and the worthless among men" and that young Athenians should study the conduct of his characters so as to seek the company of the best of men and emulate their behavior. There are few if any qualities in *The Characters* that anyone would want to cultivate.

In *The Characters* we have the warnings, the identification of habits and life choices to be avoided. It's reasonable to think Theophrastus may have written a set of virtuous character sketches as well, but they have been lost to history. Who knows, that lost booklet might be discovered one day, wrapped around some Egyptian mummy, but until then we'll have to think of our own lists of positive character types, habits, or life strategies to balance the character flaws that make up *The Characters*.

I did experiments of this sort when I first came across Theophrastus and began to look into the long chains of thought and entertainment that flowed from his miniature portraits. *The Characters* was one of the things that David McKenna and I kicked around when we were trading ideas about how stories work. As a theatre student, David knew about Theophrastus and how he influenced Greek and Roman playwrights. The first time I mentioned him, David said, "Oh yes, the Romans finally figured out how to make better characters by combining two of the Theophrastus types, and really good ones with three."

For the first time, I understood what film critics and screenwriting professors were talking about when they said characters should be "three-dimensional."

BUT WAIT — AREN'T THESE STEREOTYPES?

You can make the argument that the character types of Theophrastus are nothing but a catalogue of stereotypes. And so they have become, to some extent, simple shorthand ways of categorizing people that can sometimes obscure the real complexities of individuals. Any labels or categories we create can be used in this reductive way and we should be on guard against that.

Nonetheless, stereotypes can be useful to storytellers. They are instantly recognized by the audience, and from that point you can begin to play with them by reinforcing the stereotype, only to turn around and shatter it with some unexpected reversal of expectation. The miser can show surprising generosity when it serves some other drive in his personality, such as lust or vanity. The braggart may startle us with a moment of humility. The fierce food critic in *Ratatouille* fulfills our expectation of the "embittered critic" stereotype, but breaks out of the mold when a taste from his childhood awakens joyful memories, creating the most memorable emotional beat in the movie.

Categories and types can be used like colors in the spectrum, notes of music or letters of the alphabet. They are instantly recognized by the audience but only begin to operate at their full potential when we combine them in novel ways. Stereotypes are not always bad. They are useful for categorizing people and situations and can be used to quickly orient the audience to a character or a situation, but the real skill is in subverting them, reversing the comfortable expectations of the audience, and there can be great fun and drama in that.

A FUNNY THING HAPPENED ON THE WAY
TO THE CINEPLEX

So how did we get from Theophrastus to *A Funny Thing Happened on the Way to the Forum*?

When Sondheim, Gelbart, and Shevelove put their heads together in 1962 to create *Forum*, they were inspired by the comedies of a Roman playwright named Plautus who used stock characters like the lusty old man, the domineering wife, the clever slave, and the good-hearted prostitute, all of whom found their way into *Forum*. Plautus's plays were based in turn on the plays of a Greek named Menander who also used stock characters, derived from the work of his teacher (guess who?) Theophrastus. If there had been no Theophrastus, there would have been no Menander, no Plautus — and no *Forum*.

Menander may have studied at the Academy when Theophrastus was director. If so, while most of his classmates were preparing to be philosophers, Menander was working on a career as a comic playwright. Like George Lucas recognizing the potential in an obscure academic work called *The Hero with a Thousand Faces*, Menander knew a good thing when he saw it and began to tell stories with it. Soon after *The Characters* came into his hand, he started using the vivid, sharp-edged sketches of Theophrastus as raw material for characters in his plays. He served them up pretty much as Theophrastus had written them, as strong expressions of a certain type of behavior, without much nuance or shading.

A MIRACULOUS DISCOVERY

We know of Menander's plays mostly through fragments of papyrus mummy wrappings and Roman copies, but in 1952, by a near-miracle, an almost complete play, *The Grouch*, was discovered in a papyrus collection in Egypt. Menander seems to have been inspired by Theophrastus' sketch of "The Surly Man" to write this knockabout comedy featuring an irritable old farmer, the terror of the countryside, who chases off a young man who's been made to fall in love with his daughter by the mischievous god Pan. The old man has a change of heart when he falls into a well and is rescued by the young man, who has proven his worthiness by working on a neighboring farm. The Grouch realizes he can't get along without other people, and blesses the marriage of the young man and his daughter. The play is said to be the first to depict the phenomenon of love at first sight. Storytellers, note that its main emotional effect is a dramatic change of character, as a hard-hearted person learns to love life again with the help of a younger person. It's a device that still seems to work, winning

Oscars for Jack Nicholson and Helen Hunt in *As Good as It Gets*, and for *Up*, Pixar's animated version of the Grouch.

Jack Nicholson keeps alive the archetype of The Grouch in As Good as It Gets.

The Theophrastus-inspired plays of Menander hit a nerve in the Athenian audience. People felt the shock of recognition. Here were familiar humans with all their funny and irritating foibles. Both Theophrastus and Menander were considered daringly realistic because their character portraits, though generalized, were drawn from real life, rather than based on idealized images of gods and heroes. The myths and the tragic plays portrayed the sometimes psychotic behavior of gods and semi-divine heroes; *The Characters* and the comedies of Menander were part of a developing Greek tradition that showed the neurotic tics of ordinary men.

It may have been effective, even thrilling for a while because it was the first time these patterns of behavior had been represented on a stage, like the first time the world saw a cowboy or a mobster or a swashbuckling pirate. Menander's characters, though somewhat one-dimensional, were wildly popular and he used them over and over. As the gods and heroes formed a kind of stock company for the more serious plays about cosmic events, the Theophrastus/Menander caricatures formed a stock company for representing everyday life in a series of popular plays.

Menander's plays traveled well, for even in the provinces everyone recognized the types and found them funny. They made their way to Rome, where, tarted up a bit for the Roman taste, they played for centuries.

THE ROMAN RE-WRITE

The Roman comic playwrights Plautus, Terence, and others rewrote Menander's plays for Roman audiences and plundered his Theophrastus-flavored characters. Plautus liked the idea of a stock company of easily-recognized character types but added some new ones to the mix to represent the social world of rich Roman merchants with households full of slaves, whose agendas might be quite different from those of their masters.

Adding to the possibilities explored by Theophrastus and Menander, Plautus created a stock company consisting of:

❖ The Old Man, often a foolish old miser, called *Senex* (Latin for old man) or *Senex Iratus* (angry old man), no doubt inspired by Menander's Grouch

❖ The Domineering Wife, called *Uxor* (wife), Mulier (woman) or *Matrona* (matron)

❖ Young male lover, sometimes the miser's son, called *Adulescens Amator* (the youthful lover)

❖ The *Adulescens'* love interest, called *Virgo* (young maiden)

❖ The Cunning Slave or *Servus Callidus*

❖ The Stupid Slave, *Servus Stultus*

❖ The Maid or Nurse, *Ancilla*

❖ The Flatterer or Moocher, *Parasitus* (parasite)

- ❖ The Courtesan, *Meretrix* (harlot or prostitute)
- ❖ The Slave Dealer or pimp, *Leno* (brothel owner)
- ❖ The Bragging Soldier, *Miles Gloriosus* (boastful soldier)

You'll recognize these stock characters if you've ever seen a production of *Forum*, for it was to Plautus that Sondheim, Shevelove, and Gelbart turned for their romp through Roman comedy. I had the great pleasure of seeing *Forum* staged at the Paramount Theatre in Austin, Texas, directed by none other than David McKenna and starring our friends Jaston Williams and Joe Sears. I never laughed so hard in my life as when David's mighty, muscle-bound Miles Gloriosus opened his mouth after a bombastic triumphal entry song and sounded like Elmer Fudd, a typical McKenna touch.

Later Roman playwrights began to experiment more freely and tried combining two or more of the Theophrastus/Menander types to make a character that would no longer be one-dimensional. They found that a character who was both arrogant and cowardly made for funnier situations than a character who displayed one characteristic only, and an arrogant, cowardly and superstitious character was funnier still. They were moving towards our modern expectation that characters be nuanced and multi-dimensional.

The technique of employing stock companies of broad characters with a few easily recognized traits was just as popular in the Middle Ages, and while Theophrastus, Menander and Plautus were forgotten, their style of stock characters and situations lived on in medieval mummers' plays, miracle plays, and Commedia dell'Arte. These forms were improvisational, leaving the actors free to invent jokes and gags once they knew the broad outlines of their characters' behavior.

Theophrastus got his second wind with the invention of printing in the Renaissance. Publishers seized on *The Characters* as royalty-free, public domain content for the newly invented medium. Multiple editions appeared, translated into modern languages and illustrated with comical woodcuts showing grotesque caricatures of Theophrastus' marketplace types.

The writing of character sketches in the style of Theophrastus became a literary genre all its own. As he had satirized the tendencies of his contemporaries, eighteenth- and nineteenth-century writers mocked the standards of their times in savage sketches written in his tradition. Other writers used his types to compose plays and novels. In her last book in 1879, George Eliot turned to *The Characters* for her own essays about character, "Impressions of Theophrastus Such," written in the voice of a lonely bachelor recalling people he has known.

Theophrastus then went far out of fashion except in rarefied academic circles, but his influence can still be detected here and there. In the early 1960s three students of the great traditions of the theatre put their heads together and agreed there was comedy gold in the bawdy plays and juicy characters of the long-forgotten Roman playwright Plautus. Sondheim, Gelbart, and Shevelove were mining in a vein that had been opened twenty-three centuries earlier by a man who just kept his eyes and ears open to funny bits of behavior from the Athenian marketplace. Who knows, maybe there's more gold in Theophrastus, but perhaps his greatest gift to us as storytellers is showing us the value of close observation of human beings with all their fascinating and funny flaws.

Or in the words of "Comedy Tonight":

"Goodness and badness,
 Man in his madness,
 This time it all turns out all right,
 Tragedy tomorrow, Comedy tonight!"

An English translation of Theophrastus' *The Characters* (1902 edition by Chas. E. Bennett and Wm. A. Hammond) is available online at: *http://www.archive.org/details/charactersoftheo00theorich*

NOTE FROM McKENNA

To: The Exalted Mystic Pooh-Bah Vogler

I don't get *any* credit on this one? Great Caesar's Ghost, a lesser soul (i.e., not your best friend and collaborator) would sue you for intellectual negligence!

Allow me to remind you, dear sir, that you were obsessively kowtowing at the shrine of Joseph Campbell until I lured you away with a profusely illustrated (and damned amusing) copy of Theophrastus (hey, did I ever get that back from you?).

Kidding aside, Chris, you've performed a major excavation here. It's narrow of me, I know, but I tend to use the Theophrastus sketches for comic brainstorming, and I wonder how much modern master performers like Zero Mostel, Gene Wilder, Jackie Gleason, and Bernie Mac knew about that ancient Lesbian. Given his rogues' gallery of comically awful people, I have to believe that Jerry Stiller uses the sketches as a pillow. Molière and Shakespeare certainly knew about the grand Theo, at least as his lessons were filtered to them from centuries of theatrical tradition.

This is a much-ignored text that is reasonably available, relatively easy reading, and should be at the bedside of anyone who plans to play with story ideas. Very good of you, amigo, to give it a plug.

And hey, Vog, I should smack you around for suggesting that someone should turn this into a board game! That's the multimillion-dollar idea that was going to fund my retirement in the south of France...

CHAPTER TWELVE

THE TOOLS:
SYNOPSIS AND LOG LINE

——— McKENNA ———

As a theatre director, I have a huge advantage over other dramatic storytellers in that my script and my actors are available to me at all times. If things are getting confusing, if we don't know how it's going, if we need an overview, I can simply gather my people and get them to do a run-through rehearsal.

That run-through can be a mess (I tend to call them "limp-throughs"). We may have worked successfully on some scenes while others may be misconceived or simply unaddressed until this moment. But I'll ask my people to work through all of it so I can evaluate where we stand and what we need to do next. This "limp-through" rehearsal is a valuable tool.

Once I started screenwriting and conducting workshops for screenwriters, I searched for a tool that would be similarly helpful. I found it in work I'd been hired for years to do for film companies. It's the Synopsis and Log Line.

Film company executives solicit hundreds of scripts and books each year, far more than the executives can possibly read. So the individual executive farms out the material to "readers" who condense the pieces into book reports that describe the stories in a single sentence (i.e., the Log Line) and in a slightly more elaborate reciprocal action outline (i.e., the Synopsis). Armed with this "coverage," the executive can get a solid sense of what each script contains and can decide which deserve his or her full attention.

I began to adapt this "coverage" as a tool for myself as a writer and for my writing students. The key difference is that a "reader" is synopsizing material that already exists while a writer is synopsizing an idea that is still being created.

The tool has proven to be marvelously effective. If I am working with a co-writer, we may come to a key point of disagreement as we are hashing out our screen story. If the conflict can't be resolved, I'll suggest that either or both of us take a day to synopsize the whole story in a page or two.

Like a "limp-through" stage rehearsal, this finished synopsis lets my collaborator and me see the point of disagreement in action as it connects to the overall story design. Frequently, I'll see that my collaborator and I have slipped the tracks and are suddenly thinking very differently about the story we're creating. The synopsis lets us see clearly where that slippage has occurred and helps us to get back on track.

When my workshop writers present their ideas in synopsis form, they get to see what they know, what they don't, and where the structure needs improvement. The synopsis allows the writer to efficiently consider the entire design of the piece without having to write hundreds of pages, many of which are dead-ends.

The Log Line is equally significant. Writers write in all sorts of ways. Some need to crank out hundreds of preliminary pages to get their inspirations on the page. Others hatch the idea in outline form first. Astoundingly, Edward Albee claims that he only writes one draft of his playscripts and that they are perfect in that form.

Whatever the preliminary process, I am convinced that the writer can proceed productively only once he or she can express the overall thought in a single sentence. That sentence identifies the archetypical Hero, that Hero's "want" and the "obstacle" that Hero will battle.

This may sound harsh and restrictive until you realize that film stories are about one thing and that the Log Line clearly identifies it. For instance, *Lawrence of Arabia* is almost three hours long and deals with many issues. But the core of the piece is a Hero (T. E. Lawrence) who wants a sense of "home" and "mission" and who is torn between his native country, England, and his love for the Arabs.

Having decided on this one-sentence expression of the vast issue at hand, screenwriter Robert Bolt knew what episodes from Lawrence's life to include in his script. He also knew the overall intention that each scene in the epic script was designed to serve.

I'm including a sample Log Line and Synopsis for you to consider. It's an early draft of Ben Affleck's admirable *Gone, Baby, Gone*. Notice that the Log Line identifies the Hero (i.e., the private eye team), the "want" (i.e., to solve the kidnapping mystery) to solve the kidnapping mystery and the obstacle (i.e., the dark underbelly of the old neighborhood). It effectively describes the overall action of the story in a single sentence. Just what it's supposed to do.

Log Line: A husband and wife private eye team scours the old neighborhood when a little girl is apparently kidnapped by dope dealers.

The Synopsis isn't the story in all its detail. It doesn't outline the characters in great depth. It doesn't get into the jokes or the poignancy or the emotion of any scene. It simply pulls the spine from the script in a nearly bloodless form of writing. It's the screenwriting equivalent of an X-ray. It's meant to be a diagnostic tool, and simplicity is what we're going for.

Synopsis: PATRICK KENZIE is a happy man. He lives with ANGIE, the love of his life. They are having a kid together and are partners in a prosperous private eye firm.

They live in a tough neighborhood which is rocked by news that little AMANDA McREADY, 4, has been kidnapped. Her mom HELENE tends towards booze and dope. Helene's brother LIONEL and sister-in-law BEA hire Patrick and Angie to investigate. Cop DOYLE is willing to work with Patrick and Angie, but the case looks hopeless.

Patrick and Angie notice that local CHRIS MULLEN is in the background of all the live news reports about Amanda. Patrick and Angie check the bars where Helene hangs out to drink. Some thugs (led by RAY and LENNY) get tough with Patrick and Angie, and the heroes need to pull their guns to escape.

Cops POOLE and BROUSSARD share leads with Patrick and Angie. The cops are focusing on sex offenders LEON, ROBERTA, and CORWIN. The cops grill Helene about her relationship with Chris' dope-pusher partner CHEESE. Helene clams up, but she tells Patrick that she and thug Ray stole a fortune from Cheese.

Patrick and the cops follow this lead and discover that Ray has been tortured and killed. Helene hands the stolen loot to Patrick. Patrick and the cops hope to quietly exchange the loot for Amanda.

Patrick and Angie approach Cheese with this offer. Cheese wants his loot but he doesn't know anything about Amanda. But when another kid (SAMUEL, 12) mysteriously vanishes, Cheese calls Patrick and Angie to arrange a swap.

Doyle (his daughter was killed by kidnappers years ago) and his cops organize the swap. It's set for a remote quarry, but the deal goes awry. Gunshots are exchanged in the dark. When the dust settles, dope-pusher Chris is dead, the loot is missing and there's no sign of Amanda. Everyone assumes that Amanda has been killed.

Cheese contacts Patrick. He claims that he never had Amanda and that he certainly didn't kill her. Before Patrick can learn more, someone kills Cheese. Patrick wants to drop the case, but Angie (the investigation has caused her to miscarry) insists that he get to the bottom of things.

Patrick resists, but his lifelong pal BUBBA drags him back into the case when Bubba sells a pile of cocaine to child abusers Leon, Corwin, and Roberta. During the dope sale, Patrick sees clues connecting this trio to Samuel's kidnap.

Patrick informs Angie and the cops about this. Cop Poole barges in on the sex offenders, but he gets shotgunned to death. Patrick jumps into the fray. He kills the three sex offenders and discovers the tortured corpse of little Samuel.

Patrick is disgusted by everything he's seen. But he's forced to continue investigating when he catches cop Broussard in a lie which suggests that Broussard had a hand in killing Ray and in stealing Cheese's dope loot. This discovery forces Patrick and Broussard into a shootout. Patrick is forced to kill Broussard.

The case seems to be closed, but Angie can't let it go. She insists that she and Patrick investigate cop Doyle. They hunt Doyle down and discover that he has both the stolen loot and little Amanda (alive and well) who will replace his own murdered child.

Patrick and Angie face a tough choice. Doyle has kidnapped the child and should be punished. But Doyle will clearly be a far better parent to Amanda than dope-addled Helene. They decide to let Doyle get away with his crimes for Amanda's sake.

The Synopsis and Log Line can be invaluable in helping storytellers see the points they need to make in order to clearly grab and hold their audiences. It's a great tool.

THINGS TO THINK ABOUT

1. Read a script (they can be downloaded from any number of websites) and write a coverage report that concentrates on the Log Line and Synopsis. Be aware that "shorter is better," so work to synopsize the story in no more than two pages.

2. Take a story you are hatching and express it as a Log Line and Synopsis.

NOTE FROM VOGLER

Log Line and Synopsis are the daily tools of the story analyst's trade. In the studio system it's called the Log Line because you need a short description of the plot or concept to be entered into the studio's "log book" of stories submitted for consideration. You might find three or four stories in the log book under the title "I Married a Dolphin" so it's useful to have a short description of each so you can tell them apart.

A well-written logline can serve another purpose, possibly igniting interest in the story among the development executives, producers, directors, and actors who will read the coverage. An exciting or intriguing log line is an important element of "good coverage" that helps sell an idea to a studio's players.

David is right in encouraging you to get your story cooked down to one good sentence. However, in my studio role I have always allowed myself two or three sentences for the log line, roughly corresponding to the first, second, and third acts of a three-act structure. My log lines tended to be structured along the following lines:

> A carefree young man wins a ticket on a luxury liner and finds himself falling in love with a passionate young woman being forced to marry a wealthy man. The jealous wealthy man and his henchman make life dangerous for the lovers until the ship hits an iceberg and they all have to fight for their lives. Amidst terrible death and destruction, the young man sacrifices himself to save his lover and urges her to live life for the both of them.

This can be an effective technique for pitching a story verbally, giving the listener clear orientation about the three big movements of the story.

I think you should be able to tell your story in one sentence *and* in three sentences. In fact, you should be prepared to tell your story at any length — that's what a storyteller does. In the course of selling an idea, you will have to be able to express it as one word, one phrase, one sentence, one paragraph, one page, a three-page synopsis, a ten-page outline, or a treatment of twenty to fifty pages, all the way up to a full screenplay or novel.

Synopsis is one of those words we inherited from the Greeks, meaning "general view" or "overview." I agree with David that writing a synopsis of your work, or of a story you are considering, is one of the most valuable things you can do to really feel you "possess" the story. It can reveal plot holes, logic problems, and false assumptions that you can't see when you are working at the level of scenes, shots, and lines of dialogue. You really can't see the forest for all the trees in the way, and so you have to step back to the overview level to see how the major parts of your story relate to one another to create an overall effect. Many times doing that process has revealed a significant weakness in the story that was invisible at the scene level. In different cases, writing a synopsis has revealed that an interesting character solves an external problem but in the end has not faced an important test of character, or that the hero acts inconsistently or fails to act decisively at the critical moment. Synopsize a movie, novel or comic book you've enjoyed and I think you'll be surprised by how much it tells you about how the writer crafted the story. Synopsize your own story and you may find cause-and-effect relationships or patterns that you have missed.

CHAPTER THIRTEEN

PROPPING IT UP OR VLADIMIR PROPP'S FAIRY TALE APPROACH

 VOGLER

Now I'm going to tell you about an obscure academic work of 1920s Russian Formalist theory by a man named Vladimir Yakovlevich Propp (1895-1970). Before you run screaming from the room, I promise you'll find it entertaining and that it will change the way you look at stories. For Propp is really talking about something very simple and dear to most of us, fairy tales. We all understand them intuitively, but Propp was one of the first to think about them systematically, examining their inner processes by asking simple questions. How are fairy tales made? What are the essential pieces that allow storytellers all over the world to arrange them in endlessly varied patterns that can still be understood by everyone?

When I worked for Disney Animation I was asked to evaluate many fairy tales, both in their "raw" state and after they had been "cooked" into treatments or scripts by contemporary writers. I needed a key to break the code of fairy tales, something similar to Joseph Campbell's analysis of hero myths. Many of the things Campbell described could also be found in the fairy tales, but they were clearly a distinct form and obeyed their own rules.

The code for fairy tale construction eluded me until I stumbled on Propp's book *Morphology of the Folktale*. Propp belonged to a school of literary theory called Russian Formalism which tried to apply some principles of science to the study of literary forms. Formalists ignored psychological or poetic interpretations in favor of simply looking at the forms themselves, cataloguing and classifying the devices used by the writers as if studying organs of the body or a type of insect. Propp was interested in form and function, and he asked the same questions over and over — what are the patterns and why are they there? What function do common literary devices serve in a narrative?

Propp applied his Formalist approach to a sampling of about one hundred Russian fairy tales which had been collected from oral storytellers by the folklorist Alexander N. Afanasyev (1826-71), the Russian answer to the Brothers Grimm.

Propp claimed to see repeating patterns in the tales, involving recurring operations or functions, many of which were arranged in pairs. He identified thirty-one of these functions, which make interesting parallels to the elements of the Hero's Journey.

I believe a visit to Propp's way of looking at stories is a worthwhile stop on the path for anyone trying to master storytelling. As folklore scholar Allen Dundes suggests in his introduction to *Morphology of the Folktale*, Propp's approach could be applied not only to fairy tales, but to other narrative forms:

> "Culture patterns normally manifest themselves in a variety of cultural materials. Propp's analysis should be useful in analyzing the structure of literary forms such as novels and plays, comic strips, motion-picture and television plots, and the like." (Alan Dundes, Introduction to the Second Edition of *Morphology of the Folktale* [Austin: University of Texas Press, 1968], pp. xiv-xv)

Amen to that. Propp's functions, like Campbell's Hero's Journey and other patterns in this book, offer another blueprint for structure, another kind of logic for building narratives, and one more set of keys for opening up the mysteries of story.

PROPP'S FUNCTIONS

So what is the essence of Propp's work? In his sampling of 103 Russian fairy tales he claimed to detect thirty-one story "functions" or significant actions done by the characters. We'll examine them one by one, comparing them to the twelve Stages of the Hero's Journey and trying to identify what purpose they serve in the inventory of the storyteller.

Note that of the fairy tales that Propp dissected, not one had all of these stages in exactly the order he outlined. They all omitted one or more of the functions or arranged them in a different order, a hint of the flexibility of Propp's system. It's not a master plot for a perfect fairy tale, but rather a compendium of possibilities gleaned from a large sampling.

(Footnote to those of an academic persuasion: Propp uses two completely different systems for lettering and numbering his functions. One of them, employing both Greek and Latin letters, is too complicated to explain here. Fortunately he also used a simple system of Roman numerals which we will follow.)

As you read over these functions, compare them to a story you are working on or to a movie, play or novel you have seen or read. Do you recognize any of Propp's functions in that story? Do the functions suggest devices that you could use in your own storytelling?

PROPP'S FUNCTIONS COMPARED TO THE STAGES OF THE HERO'S JOURNEY

The Initial Situation: There's a family or a hero living somewhere.

What Propp calls "the initial situation" is the naming of the hero, the statement of his place in a family, or the naming of his occupation. Obviously this is in the Hero's Journey territory of the Ordinary World, setting a stage and introducing a character. We have to know the story is about someone from somewhere.

I.   **Absentation:** "What's missing from this picture?" A member of the family is dead, kidnapped or lost. Something's missing from the hero's life.

Hero's Journey (HJ) equivalent: The Ordinary World

This fairy tale element seems to fulfill the function of creating sympathy for the hero who might be orphaned, abandoned, lost or simply sad to see a family member go. Stories from the *Odyssey* to *Finding Nemo* have started with a family member leaving home, triggering the restless energy of the story. Stories seem to crave the completion of a family, as Bruno Bettelheim pointed out. Fairy tales like "Snow White," "Cinderella" and "Puss in Boots" begin with the death of a family member, automatically making us concerned for the welfare of the hero.

II.   **Interdiction:** Someone tells the hero "Whatever you do, don't…" (open the door, go into the woods, etc.)

HJ equivalent: Call to Adventure

I see this function and the following as forms of Call to Adventure and Refusal of the Call. Under Refusal I describe this plot device as "The Law of the Secret Door," which is that anything a hero is told not to do, he must inevitably do. (This law, like Propp's Interdiction, also works in reverse: Anything the hero is specifically told to do, he must fail to do.)

Hitchcock's films often have the hero commit some small transgression early in the story that casts a slight shadow of guilt on him, which seems almost to trigger the life-threatening complications of the plot.

(Note: Functions II and III are the first of several linked pairs found by Propp, functions that are connected by a chain of cause and effect. They operate like triggers in the design of a computer game: If Condition A is met, Action B is automatically triggered. In fact Propp's system makes a good engine for generating storylines for computer game scenarios.)

III. **Violation of interdiction:** "You're not the boss of me." The hero does exactly what has been forbidden, or fails to do something he's been told to do.

HJ equivalent: Refusal of the Call

In contemporary stories this compulsion to ignore warnings can be a quirk of character, a general resistance to authority or a sense of mischief, but in the fairy tales the heroes may simply get distracted and forget about the warning. Some, like Pandora, are compelled to break the rule by their curiosity.

"I Feel a Disturbance in the Force"
Although Propp doesn't specifically say so, the violation of the interdiction or warning seems to trigger the alertness of the villain. The small error of the hero in breaking an injunction seems to get the villain's attention, leading indirectly to a greater evil committed by the villain. Some Russian fairy tale villains have an exaggerated sense of smell and immediately go sniffing like bloodhounds after the hero, as if in reaction to some minor disturbance of their web of evil.

IV. **Reconnaissance:** "Fee fi fo fum, I smell the blood of an Englishman." The villain, perhaps tipped off by Function III, seeks information about the hero. (Or the hero may seek information about the villain. Somebody's interested in somebody else.)

HJ equivalent: Could be part of Call to Adventure or Tests, Allies, Enemies

A striking example of a villain's Reconnaissance is the Nazi officer seeking fugitive Jews in the opening sequence of *Inglourious Basterds.*

The villain (Christoph Waltz) makes a memorable Act One reconnaissance in Inglourious Basterds.

In the grammar of modern narrative the villain may not make an entrance until late in the first act or early in the second, but will often send emissaries to keep tabs on the hero, or will employ scouts who detect the hero's presence.

Propp acknowledges that the function of Reconnaissance may also be performed by a hero seeking information about the villain (Clarice Starling in *Silence of the Lambs* seeking insight into the mind of the serial killer) or by "other persons" seeking information about the hero or villain, such as a detective or investigator who stands between the hero and the villain.

V.   **Delivery:** "Enemy in sight, sir." The villain gets information about the hero. Or the hero gets information about the villain, perhaps brought by an informant.

HJ equivalent: Call to Adventure or Tests, Allies, Enemies

At some point the villain has to know the hero exists, and vice versa.

Note that IV and V form another linked pair. Propp says these functions may be represented efficiently by bits of dialogue. A greedy official may ask "Where do you get these precious stones?" and a peasant answers "Oh, a hen lays them for us."

The hero may find the information he was seeking about the villain, or the villain's inquiries may tip off the hero to the danger. The overall purpose of these two elements is to make a connection between the hero and the villain. The audience needs to know one is aware of the other.

VI.   **Trickery:** "Let's put one over on him." The villain uses information to deceive or entrap the hero, or to steal something.

HJ equivalent: Tests, Allies, Enemies

The villain may assume a disguise or take on a new form, i.e., Shapeshift. The beautiful Queen in *Snow White* transforms herself into an old woman to offer a poisoned apple to the girl. He or she may try to persuade the hero to do something, or may use magic or force directly by casting a spell or giving a sleeping potion. The Witch in *The Wizard of Oz* casts a spell to knock out the heroes with a field of poppies. The villain may set a trap or re-arrange signs to mislead the hero.

In the Hero's Journey model I have placed scenes of this type early in the second act, but as Propp suggests, they may occur much earlier in the story as part of Act One.

VII. **Complicity:** "You've made a fool out of me." The hero is tricked, or unwittingly helps the enemy.

HJ equivalents: Tests, Allies, Enemies and/or Approach

Propp's Complicity corresponds to the parts of the Hero's Journey where different aspects of personality are being explored and tested. The hero may be tricked into thinking an enemy is actually an ally, and may even be tricked into helping the enemy for a while before realizing the truth. VI and VII are proof of the hero's innocence, and techniques for winning the sympathy and identification of the audience. The horror of *Rosemary's Baby* is derived from the fact that Rosemary is tricked into bearing the Devil's child and loving it. The Wicked Queen gets Snow White to bite into the apple of her own accord. According to some lore (and Stephen King's *Salem's Lot*), vampires can only enter a victim's bedroom when invited by the victim.

VIII. **Villainy or Lack:** "Now it's personal." The villain does harm to the hero or someone close to him or her; or something vital to the hero and the hero's world is missing.

HJ equivalents: Call to Adventure, Crossing the Threshold

Propp maintains that this function and the next three, numbers VIII-XI, form a unit that he calls "Complication," saying the sequence may occur in the body of the story or at the very beginning.

On Villainy
Propp makes an important point here by noting that stories need either an evil deed or a harmful lack to drive them. Aware of his insight, I worked the concept of Lack into my approach to the Hero's Journey model.

I didn't call out a specific place in my structure for the villain's primary act of villainy, except as a possible Call to Adventure, where an initial act of villainy may be the catalyst that upsets the hero's world and triggers the adventure. In some cases the villain doesn't strike until Crossing the Threshold, where the evil deed is the final straw that propels the hero into the adventure.

In practice, the villain's act of violence or evil can be performed at almost any point in a story structure, even before the birth of the hero, if it's an action that negatively affects the hero's life. Some villains are still throwing daggers at the hero in the final scenes.

On Lack

Propp discovered that some tales in his sampling had no detectable villain, and yet the hero had to struggle against something, a condition that he calls Lack. The absence of something in the hero's life or in his community motivates the hero and the tale to action, striving to find, win back, replace, rescue or restore the missing element. In different fairy tales, a loved one is kidnapped, enchanted or lost, the hero needs a horse or a sword, or the people are starving in a famine.

The Hero's Journey approach acknowledges the concept of "Lack" as an essential element of stories and main characters, usually felt early in the story as an aching absence in the life of the main character, or perhaps a missing element in a family or society.

Love stories and family dramas may be Lack-driven and have no real villains, though there is usually someone in the cast who can temporarily play that role. Darren Aronofsky's film *The Wrestler* is a story that does very well without a formal villain to aim blows at the protagonist — he does a good job of that himself. The Lack that causes the hero to struggle in that story is the absence of an authentic family life.

IX. **Mediation, the Connective Incident:** "Obi Wan Kenobi, you're my only hope." A "dispatcher" makes misfortune or lack known to the hero; the hero is approached with a request for help, sent on a mission by the "dispatcher," or released from captivity.

HJ equivalent: Call to Adventure, Meeting with the Mentor

Propp identifies two logical steps in the progression of a story: one, the hero must be made aware of the lack or villainy, and two, the hero must be called, sent or released into the adventure to redress the lack or villainy.

Dispatcher = Herald: Propp's Mediation corresponds well with Hero's Journey Stage Two, the Call to Adventure, with Propp's "dispatcher" carrying out the same action as the Herald archetype.

In some cases the character who fulfills the Mentor role or who performs Propp's "Donor" function (see function XII) may also be the Dispatcher or Herald.

X. **Beginning Counter-Action:** "Count me in. Someone's got to do it." Usually a verbal declaration of the hero's intent, e.g., "Permit us to go in search of your princess."

HJ equivalent: Crossing the Threshold

This is the necessary moment where the hero commits to the adventure or is tossed into it. There may be lines of dialogue that announce this development, but in the visual language of movies it can be more effective to simply show heroes setting out or making preparations that make it clear they are beginning their "counter-action." Music may also signal the real beginning of the adventure, with the call of horns or drums in a new, insistent rhythm.

XI. **Departure:** "Wagons, ho!" The hero leaves home to undertake the adventure.

HJ equivalent: Crossing the Threshold

It's not enough for the hero to simply declare an intention to go forth; he or she must be seen actually going. This element is extremely important in film narrative and is usually emphasized with a strong musical cue that signals the audience that a big change is sweeping us into a new world, accompanied by visuals of the hero traveling or else arriving in the new world.

XII. **First function of the Donor:** "Are you up to the task?" The hero meets a "Donor" who first tests or questions him, perhaps even attacks him.

HJ equivalents: Combines elements of Call to Adventure and Meeting the Mentor

"Mentor," "Donor," and "Wise Old Man or Woman" are different ways of identifying someone who aids the hero by giving something necessary to achieve the quest, be it weapons, magic, wisdom, training or guidance. Some stories don't have a character that fulfills this purpose, but the function is often performed anyway by something in the hero's own character — his or her own intuition or past experience, or an "internal guidance system" such as a strong code of ethics.

Mentors/Donors are usually kind to the hero but as Propp notes, they may sometimes appear fierce at first, attacking or challenging the hero as a test of readiness or worthiness. Rafiki, the shamanic mentor of Simba in *The Lion King*, bonks the hero on the head a few times to test him, before granting the Donor's gift of a vision of his dead father.

XIII. **Hero's Reaction:** Either "I'm not quite ready" or "What are we waiting for, let's go!" The hero passes the test, or else fails temporarily. It might take three tries, but he or she passes the test eventually.

HJ equivalent: Refusal of the Call

This event seems to be needed in stories to prove that the adventure is difficult and consists of making a series of tough choices and mastering challenging skills. In those cases when the hero temporarily fails the test or refuses the Call, the delay creates some moments of suspense. Will the hero accept the challenge or pass the test, thereby winning magical aid? Is the hero ready and worthy, and if not, what is needed to make him or her ready?

XIV. **Receipt of a Magical Agent:** "Here's something to help you on your journey." The hero receives weapons, equipment, magical powers or transportation from the Donor, or wins the support of an ally or helper.

HJ equivalent: Meeting the Mentor or Tests, Allies, Enemies

Propp's use of the term "Donor" clarifies the real function of Mentors in the Hero's Journey. The essence of their job, the verb that most accurately expresses it, is "to give." They give the hero whatever is needed, be it money, advice, information, reassurance or love. This could be a passing phase, a fleeting gesture for a character who wears some other archetypal hat in the rest of the story. Even an adversary could temporarily act as a Donor, although there is usually something nasty concealed in the gift (e.g., the Wicked Queen's gift of an apple to Snow White).

This function can spill over into Tests, Allies, Enemies because what the hero wins from the Donor is sometimes an introduction to potential Allies. The Donor gives the hero the use of a magical horse or connects him to a person with magical powers who becomes a loyal Ally through the remainder of the story.

XV.   **Guidance:** "Follow the Yellow Brick Road!" The hero is transported or guided to a new land where lies the object of his search.

HJ equivalents: Crossing the Threshold and/or Approach

A hero might receive this kind of guidance at many possible junctions — upon leaving home for the first time, after meeting a Donor and winning a magical gift, or at any point in the story when the hero needs to be transported to a faraway place. Sometimes there is a journey to the edge of the Special World, then a further journey to reach the entrance (HJ Approach) of a guarded place in its center (HJ Ordeal) and yet another journey to return with a reward (HJ The Road Back). The Donor/Mentor or Ally may guide the hero, or the magical gift itself (a magic carpet, a flying horse, the Batmobile) may be the mode of transport. The Good Witch tells Dorothy to "Follow the Yellow Brick Road!"

XVI.   **Struggle:** "Only one of us comes out of here alive." The hero and villain do battle, match wits, play cards, etc. or the hero struggles to replace what is lacking.

HJ equivalent: Ordeal

A struggle, a game, a contest, a wrestling match or a tug of war between two well-matched opponents is the essence of entertainment, and can hold our attention like nothing else. Our instinctive sense is that if a narrative doesn't have something of this nature in its center, it's not a very good story. Though Propp doesn't specify what kind of struggle, we know it should be for high stakes, usually life and death. If there is no actual villain to struggle with, then heroes will contend with the Lack or the forces that resist them, and that struggle will bring the heroes to the edge of death.

XVII. **Branding:** "Ouch!" The hero is visibly wounded in the battle, or is branded or marked somehow after the battle, or receives a token like a ring or a scarf, which will later prove his victory.

HJ equivalent: Ordeal or Reward

This is a most interesting feature of fairy tales, echoing the mythic motif of the wounded hero, like one-eyed Odin or lame Oedipus. These visible signs of injury underscore the seriousness of the adventure, and may be symbolic of the hero's inner transformation or transfiguration. They serve a practical function in the plot, helping to identify the hero as the true victor in the battle when doubt is cast on his claims later in the story.

Physical tokens like rings and scarves serve the same purpose, though they are less dramatic than a physical wound. In some myths, the equivalent is a magic sword that the hero is able to seize after killing a dragon. A "brand" may also be a flaming torch that a hero picks up to light the way out of the cave.

XVIII. **Victory:** "Breathe your last, villain!" The villain is defeated. In some of Propp's fairy tale samples the original villain is killed or neutralized but is replaced by a second villain.

HJ equivalent: Ordeal, Resurrection

In modern stories our primary villains may have a life-threatening confrontation with the hero at the midpoint Ordeal, but they usually survive to face the hero again at the climax (HJ Resurrection) where they will be finally defeated. However, the hero might enjoy a partial Victory over the villain or his agent at the halfway point. We might think the villain is dead, only to discover later he has survived by some trick.

In Propp's sample of Russian fairy tales were a number of examples in which there were two villains — the original adversary and a second villain or rival, a false claimant who appears rather late in the story to dispute the hero's claim of having defeated the first villain. This creates suspense and complication, and sets the stage for the popular fairy tale motif of the three impossible tasks, which are imposed by the princess or her father to prove who is worthy.

We don't use the second villain ploy very often in modern stories, unless in romantic ones where an old flame may flare up just before the wedding to test the bond between the bride and groom. Most stories set up a single strong antagonist and let him or her harass the hero from start to finish. However, the occasional thriller may use Propp's second villain as a surprise. In *Body Heat* the main character kills a powerful man at the midpoint Ordeal but then learns in the third act that his real opponent is the man's wife who planned to frame him for murder.

XIX. **Liquidation** (of lack or injury): "Happy days are here again." The harm done by the villain is healed or whatever was lacking is restored.

HJ Equivalent: Reward, Return with the Elixir

This function is similar to the Reward phase of the Hero's Journey, where mythic heroes claim a weapon or a treasure from the hoard of a defeated dragon, and to the Return with the Elixir, where heroes bring back something from the Special World that has been sorely missed in the Ordinary World.

Propp's highly flexible model allows for stories to end at this point with the initial problem solved. However, he notes that many stories gather themselves for another burst of narrative, continuing the tale to describe the hero's difficulties in claiming his Reward and winning love. If Function XIX is the end of the story, the Liquidation should completely heal the damage caused by the villain or fill the void caused by the Lack. There should be a satisfying feeling of poetic justice, the sense that the punishments fit the crimes and the rewards and compensations are appropriate to the injuries. Any deviation from these equations will feel wrong and unsatisfying to the audience.

XX.   **Return:** "We're almost home." The hero heads for home, or for the court of a king.

HJ equivalent: The Road Back

Stories need to articulate the moment when the hero turns his or her back on the Special World and commits to going home or completing the quest. It's the mirror image of the Threshold Crossing at the end of the first act. This can be a verbal statement of intent to finish, or simply the realization that it's time to pack up and head for home. A rousing music cue will often intensify the energy in a movie at this point. There should be a sense of acceleration, rushing towards an inevitable climax.

XXI.   **Pursuit:** "Catch me if you can." The hero is pursued by the villain's relative or associate.

HJ equivalent: The Road Back

Chase scenes are a mainstay of action movies and since the early days of cinema have served the function of picking up the pace at a point when the audience may be getting a little tired. They create suspense and excitement, adding the entertainment of a race to the dramatic experience. The Russian fairy tales about the little girl Vasilisa have exciting chase scenes in which the cannibal witch Baba Yaga pursues her through the forest.

In *The Writer's Journey* I note a number of possibilities for pursuit. The hero and his or her companions may be pursued by the villain, or as Propp notes, by a relative or ally of the vanquished villain. But a hero may also chase a villain who is escaping or who has kidnapped someone or stolen something dear to him. A hero might also pursue a lover who has run away. In one extreme example in the classic Western *Shane*, the hero pursues the villain while a hero-worshipping little boy pursues the hero, and the boy's dog pursues the boy.

In some stories Pursuit is a quick way to get back through territory that took a long time to traverse on the outward journey. We've already seen this terrain so we can condense the return journey with a chase.

XXII. **Rescue:** "You're my hero." The hero is rescued or rescues someone.

HJ equivalents: The Road Back, Resurrection

This element can release a lot of emotional energy as anxiety about a loved one or the hero being imprisoned or endangered is suddenly relieved. It's equivalent to a resurrection or a return from the dead. A rescue in movies is usually accompanied by jubilant or triumphant music and a shift from darkness to light.

The rescue could be the climax of some stories, but more often it's an episode on the way to a final showdown.

XXIII. **Unrecognized Arrival:** "You look familiar but I can't place you." The hero is not recognized on arrival at the destination.

HJ equivalent: Resurrection

In some stories, the hero is not recognized because the harrowing adventure has thoroughly transformed him or her. They may have grown, their clothes may be tattered or exchanged for new garb, or they may be scarred in some way. A variation is that the hero is recognized, but his or her achievement is not. People who have been through a transformative experience in a special world may have trouble convincing the folks at home that anything has happened. The world shrugs off their life-changing, death-defying feats until they produce some proof.

Unrecognized Arrival creates suspense and sympathy for the heroes. After all they've been through, will they be eliminated or ignored at the finish line? That's the horrifying ending of *Invasion of the Body Snatchers* — the hero runs around screaming, correctly, that we are all doomed, but he is dismissed as a madman.

In another variant, heroes may desire to go unrecognized and therefore put on a disguise, because they would be killed if they came forward at this point, or because they need to secretly gather information before identifying themselves and confronting the villain. Quentin Tarantino goes for comedy at this point in *Inglourious Basterds* as his tough-talking Tennessee commando leader, Lt. Aldo Raine, ludicrously pretends to be an Italian to crash a Nazi movie premiere.

A hero tries to go unrecognized as he reaches his destination in Inglourious Basterds.

XXIV. **Unfounded Claims:** "Arrest that imposter and give me my rightful prize." A new villain claims credit for defeating the first villain or claims the right to marry the princess/inherit the kingdom.

HJ equivalent: Resurrection

Among the many possible final tests for the hero in the Resurrection phase is the appearance of a rival claimant or some circumstance that casts doubt on the hero's victory. Suspense and tension are increased by this last-minute obstacle. A spot for this development is embedded in the traditional wedding ceremony, where the celebrant says to the congregation if is there is anyone who has grounds to object to the wedding, "let him speak now or forever hold his peace." If the hero can stand up to this final test of false claims, he or she is truly qualified for the prize.

XXV. **Difficult Task:** "You know the drill, first one to perform three impossible tasks gets the girl." The princess
(or her father) sets a difficult task for the hero, or the
hero must compete with the false claimant to do the
task. A series of three tasks is not uncommon.

HJ equivalent: Resurrection

The climax of a story may be a complex passage in
which the hero is tested on many levels. It's fine to kill
dragons in the Special World but you may still have to
face doubts and obstacles on re-entry to the Ordinary
World, or in the court of a king that represents the
next level of the hero's development.

"Trebling" or repeating things three times is a fairy
tale device that says something is important or difficult. Three represents completeness, signifying that
the hero must master life on all its levels. The repetition also serves to create rhythm and suspense.

A set of three tasks is a good technique for fattening
up a plot, but in modern narrative we are usually trying
to accelerate at this point and introducing three obstacles at the last minute may be ill-advised. Threefold
tasks are common in fairy tales and myths around the
world and can be inserted at many points in the narrative, not just in the final movement.

XXVI. **Solution:** "I did it — with a little help from my
friends." The hero manages to perform the difficult
task(s), often with the aid of a magical helper or agent.

HJ equivalent: Resurrection

The hero could fail at this point, which would turn the
story into a tragedy. However, this outcome is rare in
fairy tales and the hero usually prevails. Sometimes the

victory is the result of calling on all the experiences of the journey. The hero shows that he or she has internalized useful qualities picked up from all the other characters encountered on the journey, proving that he or she has learned something and changed.

The hero can call on the aid of a magical helper or object at the critical moment. Han Solo shows up unexpectedly to assist Luke Skywalker in the final battle at the Death Star. An object from an earlier part of the story may turn out to be critical for the hero's success at this point, like Dorothy's ruby slippers transporting her back to Kansas.

XXVII. **Recognition:** "I knew it was you all along!" The hero is recognized because he or she was able to perform the task(s) or because someone sees the brand or token proving that he or she defeated the villain.

HJ equivalent: Resurrection, Return with Elixir

This element may be present because it fulfills a deep human wish. We all would like to be recognized and accepted for who we truly are. We are all special and unique even if the world doesn't treat us that way, and it's nice to be acknowledged for it once in a while.

Storytellers have known for thousands of years that recognition scenes can trigger powerful emotions in the characters and the audience. They were a standard feature of Greek and Roman novels and plays, as childhood sweethearts would be separated for many years, kidnapped by pirates, enslaved, etc. only to recognize one another and be united at the climax. This was a surefire emotional ploy in the format of an old TV show, *This Is Your Life*. Celebrities would be lured into the studio for a surprise review of their life stories. At the emotional climax of the show, a voice was heard from off-stage. The celebrities had to guess the identity of the speaker, who was always revealed to be a person from their past or their early career, someone they had not seen for many years. The shock of recognizing someone from long ago inevitably brought up old memories and triggered tears in the celebrities and in the audience.

There is something primal in the recognition scene, as the hero casts off a disguise and stands revealed in his or her true identity. On a psychological level, old masks of identity, illusions, and defenses are discarded so the real self can shine through.

XXVIII. **Exposure:** "We knew there was something fishy about him from the beginning." The villain fails to perform the task or otherwise is revealed to be an imposter.

HJ equivalent: Resurrection

This is the mirror image of the previous function, revealing the villain's true nature. It's a positive moment for the hero, canceling out the last threat to his or her success. It may not be necessary to expose the villain if his evil nature has been discovered earlier in the story, but there may be an equivalent neutralizing of the villain as he is disarmed, blocked or abandoned by his supporters.

XXIX. **Transfiguration:** "You look marvelous!" The hero acquires a new appearance. He or she is magically transformed or receives new garments symbolizing a new status.

HJ equivalent: Return with Elixir

Transfiguration is an outward sign of an inner change. Saints acquire a halo after a transcendent experience.

Ordinary people walk and talk differently after a brush with death or a difficult ordeal. Being a visual medium, movies often show how a character has changed by having him or her costumed and lit differently at the end of the story, as well as behaving differently.

XXX. **Punishment:** "Curses, foiled again!" The (second) villain is punished by the princess or her father.

HJ equivalent: Return with Elixir

This is going the extra mile to thoroughly defeat and humiliate the villains, required by the fairy tale's rigid sense of justice. It's not enough that they are thwarted, neutralized and exposed as imposters; they must also receive a formal sentence from the authority figures in the tale, the princess or her father the king. (This is similar to a scene of courtroom judgment that caps many legal thrillers.) Villains may be executed on the spot, stripped of honors or banished from the realm.

Because movies so often fake you out by having apparently dead villains leap back to life, you may have to really crush your villains to convince skeptical audiences they are truly defeated.

XXXI. **Wedding:** "Here comes the bride" and "They lived happily ever after." The hero marries the princess or takes possession of all or half of the kingdom.

HJ equivalent: Return with Elixir

Fairy tales and Hollywood movies specialize in happy endings, unlike myths which always seem to end badly if you follow their threads long enough. The wedding is a convenient way to close the circle of a story, showing the beginning of a new cycle. The restless energy of the story, set in motion by the disruption of a perfect, happy family in the beginning (Absentation), can finally be stilled.

Many stories end with the equivalent of a wedding as a new alliance or contract is agreed upon. "Louis, I think this is the beginning of a beautiful friendship," as Bogart says to Claude Rains at the end of *Casablanca*. Or it may be that two sides of a warring personality are now at peace, or that two conflicting ideas or ways of life have been reconciled.

In some fairy tales there is no princess to marry, and so the hero only takes possession of the kingdom or is given half the kingdom by the grateful king. Both the wedding and the hero's assumption of the throne symbolize the beginning of a new cycle and a return to the perfection that fairy tales seem to crave.

CONCLUSION

Propp only deals in what he found in his limited fairy tale sample. He does not enumerate every possible story function one can imagine, but leaves room for elements that don't fit into his perceived categories of action, labeling them "X."

We can think of many more common actions or functions that we observe regularly in stories, such as

Making a Wish
Making a Deathbed Promise
Meeting Someone to Make a Romance or Alliance
Bargaining, Making a Deal
Betraying
Bluffing
Flirting
Getting Revenge
Earning or Losing Respect
Getting an Idea
Having a Baby, etc.

Writers know these devices almost intuitively but it's not a bad idea to think systematically about them as Propp did and make our own lists of modern story functions.

Try the experiment. Brainstorm and write down as many of these common functions as you can think of. Look at a *Star Wars* movie, an episode of *Glee*, or a Harry Potter novel and try to identify the function of each scene. Is it one of Propp's thirty-one functions? Is it one from your own list? Is it unique to this story or can you think of other story examples of this particular function?

There are playful possibilities in Propp's work. Almost as soon as *Morphology of the Folktale* was translated into English, researchers used the thirty-one functions to create a computer program to generate fairy tales. You can find a Proppian fairy tale generator on the Internet at: *http://www.brown.edu/Courses/FR0133/Fairytale_Generator/gen.html*

The website simply lists Propp's thirty-one functions and allows you to check off which ones you would like to include in your story. It then generates a fresh fairy tale for you, composed of stock phrases that have been loaded into its memory. I tried it and was astonished by the variety of dramatic and poetic effects I was able to get by including or excluding certain functions.

In one experiment, I selected only functions that sounded negative to me or harmful to the hero, excluding his victories. The result was a blood-curdling Gothic tale filled with disturbing imagery, worthy of Stephen King in a particularly paranoid mood. On the opposite tack, I commanded the story genie to create me a tale composed only of events that would be positive for the hero, and the result sounded like a sappy Victorian fairy story filled with butterflies and sunshine. You can have a lot of fun generating stories and learning how the emotional feeling changes as you add or omit different functions.

Try the story generator, or create your own by writing short sentences of description matching each of Propp's functions. If you try the online fairy tale generator you'll get the idea of how it was constructed. You'll need to write two or three variations on each function to make it interesting. Then start selecting functions from Propp's list and see how your sentences of description string together to make an original fairy tale.

Propp's system of functions is far from perfect, and doesn't cover every possibility we might confront in making stories for today's readers and audiences, but it is a start at bringing a systematic approach to naming the working parts of stories. It sheds a lot of light on the inner workings of fairy tales, and can be useful as a reminder for those who are working with fairy tales or want to bring a little of the fairy tale feeling to contemporary stories. For any writer, Propp's terms can greatly increase the inventory of story possibilities and add to our awareness of the power that still lives in the old stories. Let's build on his work, collecting and identifying the story moves we use in our work, and creating as many new ones as we can possibly devise.

NOTE FROM McKENNA

Confession here: Chris has been greedily keeping Mr. Propp to himself. So, like you, I'm encountering his take on this material only now.

I'll also confess that, once I absorb his take, I have every intention of turning it into a lecture/performance piece of my own. If I'm gonna steal, I may as well steal from the best.

CHAPTER FOURTEEN

Propp on Character

VOGLER

Propp's attention to function, to how an element actually operates to advance the plot of a fairy tale, led me to a breakthrough in my understanding of the character archetypes. At first I had formed the simplistic thought that a character who expressed a certain archetype had to walk and talk in the style of that archetype throughout the story — once a mentor, always a mentor. The hero is the hero, the villain is the villain, and that's that. Propp showed me the archetypes could be viewed as temporary, transient functions or jobs to do, functions that different characters might perform as required by the story.

These functions did not have to be "stuck" to a particular character; they could be passed around like masks or hats that the characters wore as necessary to advance the plot. It suddenly made the work of conceiving characters freer. The human beings depicted in stories were free to be complete and complex individuals, who only sometimes fulfilled mythic roles ("archetypes") that they took on themselves or had projected on them by others. The archetypes could still do their job of evoking primal emotions but in a much more realistic fashion.

Propp offered a functional analysis of character, identifying seven or eight significant actions and actors essential to create a fairy tale. He defined characters solely by what they did, by what function they performed in the plot. He wasn't really talking about characters as we understand them, as multi-layered individuals, but rather as functions performed by different people to carry out necessary operations in the plot.

Propp looked at character, like everything else, through his Russian Formalist lens, and was thus concerned primarily with function. What actions are possible is more important in his theory than who does the actions. He assigned each character a "sphere of action" which consists of the typical functions that type of character can logically perform, in effect defining the characters by what they do.

1. The Villain is defined by doing evil, tricking the hero and struggling against him or her (HJ equivalent: Shadow, Antagonist, Adversary).

2. The Donor's function is to prepare the hero or give the hero some magical object (HJ equivalent: Mentor/Wise Old Man or Woman).

3. The Helper, sometimes with magical powers, aids or guides the hero in the quest (HJ equivalent: Ally). Magical objects such as flying carpets and magic powers such as invisibility operate like Helpers and follow the same rules. A character who does the Donor function may also do the Helper function.

4. The Princess may be kidnapped, imprisoned or enchanted and must be rescued by the hero (HJ equivalent: Shapeshifter). The Princess (and/or her father the King) gives the difficult task to the hero and identifies the false hero. The Princess marries the hero, and the King gives the hero all or part of his kingdom to rule. Propp insisted that functionally the princess and her father cannot be clearly distinguished and so he treats them as a single "character."

5. The "Dispatcher" makes the lack known and sends the hero off on the quest (HJ equivalent: Herald). A Donor may also perform the Dispatcher function, or there may be a separate person to do the Dispatcher job.

6. The Hero has many functions: He can break an injunction, be tricked by the villain into aiding him, react to the Donor, struggle with and defeat the villain, perform the difficult task, wed the princess, etc.

7. False Hero or Second Villain (HJ equivalent: Shadow) takes credit for the hero's actions or tries to marry the princess, and is exposed and punished.

Propp also uses the catch-all term "connections" for a class of characters who exist simply to make a necessary exchange of information. They may include "complainers, informers, slanderers" who bring knowledge of a problem to the hero or bring information about the hero to the villain.

Propp isn't interested in who does the action — that may change from tale to tale, being done by a princess in one tale, a king in another, a witch in a third — but in the action itself. He was looking at the verbs, always a good idea for screenwriters and writers in general. The verbs carry the action. Strong, simple, functional verbs make good writing. Thinking as Propp does, defining characters by what they do, can help make your writing leaner and more focused on action.

CHAPTER FIFTEEN

ENVIRONMENTAL FACTS: OVERVIEW

——— McKENNA ———

ENVIRONMENTAL FACTS

Chris has been describing the Twelve Stages of a story for years. It's a valuable tool for me as a theatre director, story analyst, script doctor, raconteur, and teacher. It's a diagnostic device that leads me to the provocative questions I need to crack almost any story I'm considering.

But this isn't the only such tool at my disposal. I want to promote another to you which takes a different angle on the challenge of telling stories. It was suggested to me by my directing mentor at the University of Texas, Francis Hodge.

Let's call this tool the Environmental Facts.

Hodge was a taskmaster, admitting students like me to the high order of directors only once we proved our worth. Before Hodge would allow me to cast actors and stage scenes for his class, he would demand that I create an exhaustive Director's Preparation.

Hodge would have me pore over my scripts to unearth their hidden secrets. He turned me into a story detective, probing deeper and deeper into the material. He would scoff at my uninformed first impulses, and he would encourage me to seek the questions that needed to be asked before the artistic work could begin in earnest.

Hodge's format was deceptively simple. He would have students write essays on each of the Environmental Facts. These facts were the Date, Location, Social Environment, Political Environment, Religious Environment, and Economic Environment.

It was important that we begin by writing an individual essay on each of these topics rather than to create one cohesive, integrated overview. Writing that many essays seemed counter-productive, but I discovered after the fact that comparing and contrasting the details from the various essays would expose recurring factors. Paying attention to these recurring factors would lead me to the storytelling gold I was seeking: the hidden questions that needed to be asked.

It was tedious work, and I resented it. But after I submitted to the grind of it, I slowly developed a precise understanding of what I was doing. I was better equipped for the job of interpreting plays than I could have previously imagined.

WHAT I DISCOVERED

With Hodge holding my feet to the fire, I learned some-thing basic about playscripts and screenplays. I came to see that a writer imagines a full dramatic event in three dimensions. The writer then applies art and craft to transform that three-dimen-sional experience into a two-dimensional document: a script.

This is a tricky matter because the third dimension gets lost unless the writer successfully imbeds effective clues about it in the script.

Where do we find these clues? They are usually folded into the implicit Environmental Facts. It's up to skilled interpretive artists (actors, directors, designers) to identify, understand, and then revive the third dimension as they stage the script.

By making me deeply analyze the script, Hodge forced me to reshape myself into a story detective, capable of reading the clues and drawing inspired conclusions from them.

What sorts of things was I looking for? Well, I knew that I'd have to examine the various characters' "wants," and that I would prosper by identifying the obstacles the characters face. I knew that I could examine the Reciprocal Actions of each scene to identify the conflicting Polarities in operation.

Did I have a tool to help me do this? Why not start by using the Log Line and Synopsis?

Hodge was making a promise. If I could correctly identify and interpret the clues exposed in my Environmental Facts essays and my investigations into "wants," Reciprocal Actions and Polarities, I would enter and understand the special three-dimensional world the writer had originally imagined. I could accurately turn the two-dimensional script into a compelling living performance.

IT WORKS BOTH WAYS

Then I realized something more astounding. The Environmental Facts tool worked in both directions!

If I mastered the tool, I didn't have to limit myself to being only a director. I could also be a creator. I could become a writer, too, knowing how to imbed the third dimension clues of my stories for other detectives to find.

Could I become a playwright or a screenwriter? Why not? At the very least, I could use the tools to entertain my friends with funnier jokes and put kids to sleep with more engrossing bedtime stories.

A NEW PERSPECTIVE

Hodge's close analysis tool opened a new perspective to me. I began to see that dramatic narrative is a game of clue detection. Hodge was telling me that directors, actors, and designers must hunt for clues hidden within the writer's two-dimensional script document. But I soon realized that audiences, too, are detectives. We read stories and watch films and plays to deduce what is happening and what may happen next. Storytellers who understand this game of clue and detection offer a special level of appeal.

The use of provocative clues encourages me as interpreter and audiences in general to invest ourselves in stories and to be transformed by them.

Hodge's painstaking exercise changed me. When I began directing, I was only imitating other people's work. After operating under Hodge, I learned how to effectively question not only scripts, but also the world at large. I was no longer taking things at face value and living on raw impulse.

OVER TO YOU

I'll take Professor Hodge's position for the moment and invite you to accept his challenge. The following chapters will walk you through the exercise of the Director's Preparation and the Environmental Facts. I'll try to get you thinking of productive questions.

After that, the tool is in your hands, and the ball is in your court. The work will be hard, but I guarantee you that it's worth doing.

THINGS TO THINK ABOUT

To activate our Environmental Facts tool, we'll investigate a script together. During our coming chapters, we'll question the given circumstances and hidden clues in the Karen McCullah Lutz/Kirsten Smith script for *Legally Blonde*.

Take a look at the script (it's accessible on the Internet) and get inquisitive. Start by doing a Log Line and Synopsis which takes the twelve stages of the Hero's Journey into account.

NOTE FROM VOGLER

Whew. I thought we'd never get here. I've been trying for years to get David to write down how he does this "Director's Prep" thing. He has many more such techniques in his tool kit but I'm quite happy to get him to cough up this one. He has a broad, well-integrated view of the world, of history, politics and sociology, and the Environmental Facts is a perfect expression of his multi-angled approach to almost anything.

CHAPTER SIXTEEN

ENVIRONMENTAL FACTS I: DATE

——— McKENNA ———

Let's get to work by considering the first of Hodge's Environments: Date.

Simply stated, the "date" is the day, month, year, season, century, and time of day during which the action of the story takes place. Sounds obvious, but there is a wealth of nuance here. A storyteller who asks good questions of his/her "date" will unearth unexpected details, compelling for both the characters and the audience.

Let's consider the concept of specific days for a moment. Anybody who holds down a regular job knows that Mondays are drudgery, that Wednesday is "hump day" and that we should all "TGIF" (particularly if it's payday). Each day has a specific quality that affects how people behave.

How about seasons? I'm not a big fan of winter, so I spend my January days longing for baseball pitchers and catchers to begin spring training. It's a promise of better times, and my spirits lift when that February day arrives. Did your villain shoot Santa on Christmas or poison the champagne on New Year's Eve? How does your romantic couple feel about Valentine's Day? The film *Sixteen Candles* revolves entirely around a forgotten birthday.

Time of day? My personal safety insists that I recognize that my Manhattan neighborhood is different at 2 PM than it is at 2 in the morning. Transylvanians don't fear Dracula until the sun goes down. What about the difference between early birds who are up and productive at the crack of dawn and night owls who only get the feel of things after dark? For 9-to-5ers, isn't there something vaguely sinister about people who work the night shift and sleep all day?

The implications of "date" extend as far as your imagination will take you. How do we react to the first day of school? To graduation day? To your wedding day? You better be ready to file on Tax Day.

Our understanding of the world would be very different if we lived before 1492 rather than after it. How about before and after 1776? Before and after the 1960s civil rights movement?

If you were a moneyed Parisian in 1785, good taste would have you dress in the king's elaborate high heels and fabulous wigs. Six years later, good sense would have you ditch those fashions so you could fit in with the guillotine-happy Revolutionary mob. On an essential level, all that happened is a date change.

In first-century Rome, Christians were being thrown to the lions. A few centuries later, they were running the place.

All Americans know the significance of "9/11."

It's all about the "date," and good storytellers know how to exploit this "fact."

Here's an example. The film classic *The Best Years of Our Lives* (screenplay by Robert Sherwood) is driven by its "date." It occurs during the months after World War II, and it deals with three American war veterans as they return home to civilian life. During the war, one of them was a glamour boy bomber pilot, pulling down top pay and soaring through the heavens. Another was an infantry sergeant, slogging through Europe in hand-to-hand combat against the Nazis. The third was a Navy machinist, a skilled technician until his hands were blown off in a sea battle.

The war specified these identities. But the times have changed, pressing our heroes into challenging new roles. Once he's home, the flyer learns that "ninety-day wonder" glamour boys are literally out-of-date. His identity is now reduced by his menial job as a soda jerk. The gung-ho sergeant returns to family responsibilities that drop him back at his bank desk job. The work offers him status but little of the adventure he's been living. The machinist is no longer in the company of wounded heroes. Once an admired figure, he chafes within a domestic world that considers him a "cripple."

The film is extraordinarily touching, and the emotion rises out of the date change.

Neil Jordan's 1986 film *Mona Lisa* (screenplay with David Leland) is all about date, too. Bob Hoskins plays a British mobster who has served his bosses by doing a stretch in prison. Back on the streets now, he should be rewarded for his devotion. But "date" has changed the environment. The old-school mobs have sold out to larger corporate interests, meaning that Hoskins' mob enforcer skills are no longer valued. Instead of being promoted, he's placed at the bottom of the corporate food chain, setting off his drama.

Dates go haywire for Marty McFly in the Robert Zemeckis/Bob Gale *Back to the Future* series. Thrown out of his ordinary time, Marty can convincingly refer to himself as "Clint Eastwood" and has to field sexy advances from the hot teen girl who happens to be his mother.

On this level, the matter of date presents an entirely new world, a new identity, and a new set of conflicts for the characters.

I mentioned day of the week as a potential factor, and that's clearly true for the hero of Nik Cohn and Norman Wexler's *Saturday Night Fever*. During the workweek, Tony delivers paint for a hardware store. But at the Saturday night disco, he is the king of the dance floor.

Time of day is a key factor for *Batman*. When the sun is up, he's wealthy philanthropist Bruce Wayne. But when criminals threaten the landscape after nightfall, our hero becomes the Caped Crusader.

Smart storytellers don't arbitrarily pick their time frames. The question of "when" offers all sorts of shadings that make a difference.

In Saturday Night Fever, *Tony's a working stiff until the weekend transforms him into a king.*

Let's not leave our "date" essay quite yet. There is another essential question to be asked that can activate the innards of the story. That question is "why this day and no other?"

This is essential because one specific incident, unusual for the key characters, frequently sets off a chain of events that forms the special arena of the drama. The date that inciting event occurs changes everything.

For instance, in *Some Like It Hot*, musicians Joe and Jerry must transform themselves into "Josephine" and "Daphne" only because they witness the St. Valentine's Day Massacre. Sharks swimming in the oceans are a non-event unless one (like "Bruce" in *Jaws*) attacks a seaside town on the 4th of July. Woodward and Bernstein in *All the President's Men* rise from the status of promising rookies to top investigative reporters only because they stumble across the Watergate break-in. Rocky is an obscure pug until Apollo Creed needs a challenger to fight. Little Elliott is an unimportant kid until E.T. crashes into his neighborhood. Sheriff Bell of *No Country for Old Men* can only wonder how he'd stack up against his lawman ancestors until the monstrously lethal Anton gives him the terrifying opportunity to find out.

All of these characters become heroes because something happens on a specific day, a day unlike any other, which forces them onto the playing field. What was life before for these people? How is that life changed because an inciting event happens to them on a specific date?

Every story you will ever tell or hear is set in some specific time (however indefinitely that "date" is stated). Explore that fact to your benefit. Ignore it at your peril.

THINGS TO THINK ABOUT

1. We're going to run the Karen McCullah Lutz/Kirsten Smith script for *Legally Blonde* through all of these Environmental Facts chapters. Get things rolling by doing an essay on the Date Environmental Fact. Meditate deeply, even consider important dates in the histories of the two major locations (Los Angeles and Cambridge). Also consider the continuing question of "why this day and no other?"

2. How does the historical date affect *Casablanca*? If you do a little research about 1942, you'll see that life very much affected art in this case.

3. What was going on in the '50s that made *Rebel Without a Cause* and *The Wild One* such sensations? Would those circumstances be the same if the date were changed?

4. Why "this day and no other" for *Scarface*? For *Dr. Strangelove*? For *What Women Want*? For *Edward Scissorhands*?

NOTE FROM VOGLER

Bravo and amen. I am always trying to get writers to be specific about dates, time of day, and especially seasons of the year, as these can be important anchors for the story, making it part of a cycle of time. The recent re-telling of *Robin Hood*, Ridley Scott's version with Russell Crowe, makes good use of a fall harvest festival to show how the whole community came together to celebrate their relief at putting away enough food to survive the winter. Also, I'm a stickler for historical accuracy or at least an authentic feeling, and I love it when writers bring in a little awareness of the context of a period piece. The casual hygiene of the surgeon Dr. Maturin in Peter Weir's *Master and Commander* is horrifying to us germ-conscious modern folk but perfectly natural in the eighteenth century.

CHAPTER SEVENTEEN

ENVIRONMENTAL FACTS 2: LOCATION

———— McKENNA ————

The old adage has it that the three most important factors in real estate are "location, location, location." The adage holds true for storytellers.

Location is the precise place where the action occurs. Exactness matters. A story might be set in Rio de Janeiro, but the atmosphere is entirely different on fabulous Ipanema Beach than in the hellish Cidade de Deus ghetto. The French film *Jean de Florette* occurs on two neighboring farms, but since one has access to water while the other doesn't, the matter of a few yards becomes the core of a compelling tragedy.

At its core, *Casablanca* is about a guy who torments the girl who dumped him. It's not much really, but the location (North Africa at the outset of World War II) elevates this minor tussle by setting it at the center of a fatally imperiled planet. By the end of the story, both guy and girl understand that "the problems of three little people don't amount to a hill of beans in this crazy world." A second-rate soap opera idea becomes one of the all-time great movies because of location.

Location opens up all sorts of possibilities for storytellers because people make unique adjustments to the places they live. I almost always have a great time in New Orleans. The natives have a peculiar accent because their town is a cultural explosion of Caribbean, Cajun, and Southern. Their sound has a "Brooklynese" quality because the city has been a major port for centuries, attracting a wide array of European and African influences.

Casablanca *may be set in a Moroccan nightclub, but this opening shot suggests that the location has far larger implications.*

As a port city, New Orleans has always been about business. So of course the locals are chatty and outgoing. It's also a great example of how the climate of a location affects costume, attitude, and all sorts of folkways. New Orleans is a steamy place much of the year, creating a casual lifestyle distinct from the greater formality you might find in colder ports like New York, Shanghai or London.

Although close in latitude to New Orleans, West Texas has an entirely different sound and approach to life. The geography (the dried-up bed of a prehistoric ocean) rivals a lunar landscape for remoteness. There are fewer people here, and they culturally resemble each other. The result? A more consistent accent than you'd hear in the motley French Quarter.

When I first heard this sound, I was intrigued by its tight-lipped, "man of few words" quality. I couldn't make sense of it until my West Texan actor buddy Jaston Williams from *Greater Tuna* explained that places like Lubbock and Alpine frequently endure unimaginable sand storms. The natives know that getting chatty will cost them a mouthful of grit. Better to keep your lips sealed and to speak only when you have something to say. Location again.

Location can establish class and economic realities. In Howard Hawks' film *Sergeant York* (screenwriters include Abem Finkel, Harry Chandlee and John Huston), Alvin and his farming kin are impoverished because they live near the top of a Tennessee mountain where the soil is thin and rocky. Hoping to marry well, Alvin begins a grand adventure to buy some fertile "bottom land." His location instigates the action.

Writer Tamara Jenkins was having a great creative day when thoughts of location led her to hatch the ironic and spot-on film title *The Slums of Beverly Hills.* Poor people in the land of McMansions? Let's run with it. This insightful, location-based wordplay tells us that we're in for a special kind of culture clash.

Location speaks to matters of politics. Just ask anyone divided by the Iron Curtain during the Cold War of *From Russia with Love* or *The Spy Who Came In from the Cold.* The Guatemalan siblings of *El Norte* have a tale to tell about their quest to enter the American Southwest.

Many Westerners can't identify the difference between Chinese and Japanese natives. But these two cultures, generated by their different locations, can be worlds apart. Filmmakers Ang Lee and James Schamus make the most of that location conflict in *Lust, Caution.*

People living in the Carolinas during the American Civil War of John Jakes' TV mini-series *North & South* face the heartbreaking decision of identifying with either their state or their country. By the way, when I moved from my New Jersey birthplace to college in Texas, I learned that Southerners refer to the Civil War as "The War of Northern Aggression." Goes to show that location molds your point of view.

Location affects religion. When European conquistadors first encountered Native Americans, they were appropriately perplexed. The Natives wore little clothing and lived communally. They had little need to venture far from the land where their gods had placed them. It was as if they were still in the Garden of Eden.

On the other hand, Original Sin and centuries of religious warfare had marked the European newcomers with an entirely different sense of this world and the next. Given this philosophical and physical disparity (all driven by the accident of location), it's no wonder that the Europeans treated the Natives like shameless savages and that the embattled Natives (like Old Lodge Skins from Calder Willingham's *Little Big Man* script) thought that Eurocentrics were insane.

The well-known "fish out of water" story model usually involves moving a character from a familiar location to a difficult new one. The major characters of *The Little Mermaid* and *Splash* know all about that as they give this story model its name. "Home-field advantage" is a sports term, but it speaks to the essence of the "fish out of water." Who in our story has the "advantage"?

One such "fish" is Joan Wilder, the novelist heroine of *Romancing the Stone*. She makes a fine living spinning romantic yarns for her readers. But she shares a solitary New York apartment life with only a cat and seems fated for spinsterhood. Fortunately, adventure calls her to real-life exploits in the jungles of Colombia where she finds high stakes and the man of her dreams. As she begins, she's new to these unfamiliar waters, and almost everyone else has the advantage over her.

Can Joan overcome her disadvantage and master her new location? I won't spoil it, but I will tell you that the climax is location-oriented in a cave called "El Corazon." Scriptwriter Diane Thomas signals to us that lovelorn romance writer Joan must journey to "The Heart" to get to the heart of the matter of matters of the heart.

Let's play with this location notion. Why not have the new surroundings come to the fish? For instance, in *The Bridges of Madison County*, Francesca begins as a farm wife living in Iowa. But she's also a displaced Italian war bride who has music in her soul. For the sake of family harmony, she suppresses her romantic appetite and comes to terms with her small pond.

She's maintaining a delicate emotional balance until her family leaves for a week. Suddenly globetrotting hunk Robert drops in on her doorstep with the waters of the outside world in one hand and a taste for sensual melody in the other. Will Francesca remain true to the limitations and family pleasures of Iowa? Or will she become a flowering Italian romantic again? Where is her "home field"? Can she construct a private location that fulfills all of her natures?

Location can address style and theme. George Lucas dramatized the peak experiences of his hot-rodding California childhood in *American Graffiti*. But when he sought to transform those experiences into grand mythology, he needed the larger scale of "a long time ago in a galaxy far, far away." Lucas's unique *Star Wars* location elevates Luke Skywalker's rite of passage and his lessons about how the world works.

Is there an old story you want to re-tell? Why not re-energize it with a location change? That's just what writer-director John Carpenter did during his 1970s salad days. He wanted to make a Western in the mode of what Howard Hawks did with the Jules Furthman/Leigh Brackett *Rio Bravo* script. Carpenter's budget was tiny and John Wayne wasn't available to him. So he reinvented the story by locating it in a modern urban setting.

Assault on Precinct 13 is *Rio Bravo* re-mixed, retrofitting the conventions of Hawks's classic western with the working machinery of a contemporary thriller. As the '70s moved on, Westerns were declared "dead." But dozens of other storytellers followed Carpenter's lead, making urban cop stories the new Wild West.

Sex and the City is all about a magical New York where 30-something women of adventure live out fabulous experiences while working as part-time newspaper columnists, etc. The series ended, but producers knew they had tapped a demographic gold mine. So ABC-TV transformed the gals into *Desperate Housewives* (*Sex and the Suburbs?*). The impulses were the same, but the setting changed the meanings.

You get the idea. Ask good questions of location, and your stories will be richer for it.

THINGS TO THINK ABOUT

1. Do another *Legally Blonde* essay, this time concentrating on the location. There's the obvious transfer of the action from Los Angeles to Cambridge, but consider, too, the significance of the classrooms, dorm rooms, sorority houses, beauty salons, prisons, courtrooms, and legal offices.

2. Consider the first pages of a piece you're writing. Are you making the most of your location? What can you do to better bring your location to life and to have it affect the players in your story?

NOTE FROM VOGLER

David mentions *Romancing the Stone* for its effective use of locations. Here's a film we judged differently at first. He loved it right away; I was scornful of it, thinking it was too slick and cartoonish. In truth, I was jealous of the seeming overnight success of the screenwriter, Diane Thomas, and it clouded my judgment. In hindsight I have come to see it as a brilliant script, filled with clever touches. The locations are used effectively to create exciting action scenes and symbolize developments in the main character, and the contrast between the heroine's Ordinary World in New York and the exotic Special World of Colombia is especially vivid.

CHAPTER EIGHTEEN

ENVIRONMENTAL FACTS 3: SOCIAL ENVIRONMENT

 McKENNA

The next four Environmental Facts chart an area of great subtlety and opportunity. Subtlety because the terms and concepts can get slippery. Opportunity because we can open our minds widely here to consider all sorts of far-flung information. Our Environmental Fact essays aren't looking for a single "right answer." We are exploring informational threads that we can weave into our overall story design. We are looking for the hidden questions that need to be asked.

Let's go "macro" for a minute, start our Social Environment meditation at the roots of human society. Our prehistoric ancestors experienced constant danger, were subject to hostile climates and faced ferocious enemies. In order to secure food, water, shelter, and (most importantly) protection, our ancestors banded together into societal packs. Humans evolved, and the social order of these packs evolved along with them.

This deep background suggests that society is an association individuals construct for mutual survival. We inhabit such associations (giving up some personal freedom in the process) so that we can reasonably anticipate common behavior. We accept unspoken rules, perform duties, and enjoy rights forged by the cohesion of the social group.

WHAT IS THE "GLUE" THAT HOLDS SOCIAL GROUPS TOGETHER?

Use yourself as a starting line. Do you belong to clubs? Are you a member of a church organization? Are you politically active? Who are your Facebook friends? Who's in your phone's "favorites" list? What do these choices say about your social orientation?

A specific geographical location may generate a social identity. On that level, Texans are very different from New Englanders, and the customs of rural churchgoers can be at odds with those of agnostic city folk.

Ethnicity is another form of social glue. So are class and financial status. All three affect the fish-out-of-water comedy for Eddie Murphy and Dan Aykroyd in *Trading Places*.

So can we assume that group security is a focal value of the social environment? Are there other values? How about groups that provide their members with points of identity? People seeking identities in this way can become Toronto Maple Leaf fans or medical students or computer geeks or Star Trekkers. We might band together as "right to lifers" or suburbanites or opera lovers. Does it matter whether your cell phone is Verizon or AT&T? The corporations promoting these products certainly hope to inspire a group identity.

Let's investigate social groups that have specific functions. If your family moves into a new neighborhood, people from down the street or from the local church or from a political party might come by with a "welcome wagon" cake and information about how things are done here. A similar orientation ritual happens every fall for incoming college freshmen.

New members of the military should expect a harsher orientation experience because rigid discipline and common cause are key factors to military success. Different group functions lead to different social rituals. Why must immigrants seeking citizenship in the U.S. pass tests about their adopted homeland?

SUBTLE SOCIAL CUES

Bear in mind that the process of being part of a social group isn't always so explicit. All sorts of enigmatic and implicit folkways rule social communities. Consider something as simple as a public greeting. In American society, socially acceptable men may shake hands while female acquaintances may exchange a peck on the cheek. Wouldn't such a peck between men inspire gossip and reproach? That peck between women passes without comment, but a kiss on the lips (a matter of mere millimeters) has an entirely different social meaning. It depends upon the social and sexual orientation of the group, right?

So when we probe the social environment, we are wise to account for details like education, class, income, intelligence, race, religion, sexual orientation, political affiliation, age, ethnicity, and marital status. Using these details, we must question the social expectations connected to these distinctive groups.

SOME EXAMPLES

Let's apply a few examples to our assumptions. In short, what social environment rules our story?

Charles Lederer's 1962 version of *Mutiny on the Bounty* is a clear-cut case, featuring an astonishing clash of social expectations. Eighteenth-century English sea captain Bligh hopes to win the favor of the King of Tahiti so he can complete a business deal. So Bligh commands his officers to behave like gentlemanly diplomats when dealing with the King's subjects. Bligh grows alarmed when he sees that the King's daughter has sexual feelings for junior officer Fletcher Christian. To avoid a business catastrophe, Bligh orders Christian to remain on the ship for the duration of the visit.

This seems like the logical and socially correct response. But Bligh, responding to his own social environment, is failing to observe the unique social priorities of Tahiti. The King rules a remote island with a limited gene pool. As such, he welcomes an infusion of fresh blood from visitors. To the King, Bligh's discreet removal of Christian is an insult that nearly ends the business negotiation. When Bligh sees his social gaffe, he is forced to officially order Christian to make love to the King's daughter.

Business deals in England get settled with a handshake. Much to his chagrin, Mutiny on the Bounty's Captain Bligh learns that Tahitians demand he shake something else.

The matter of social environment is pretty obvious in this case, but it plays a role in almost every story. "Fish-out-of-water" stories thrive on such social conflicts. In *The Devil Wears Prada*, recent graduate Andrea must adapt to the social order of the pressurized fashion world if she wants to hold down her new job. In *Enchanted* the social expectations of heroine Giselle's fairy tale world comically collide with the realities of New York City. In *The Graduate*, Benjamin's East Coast college education prepares him poorly for the society of upscale Southern California where "plastics" is a magic word and where Mrs. Robinson has unexpected power.

In *Almost Famous*, the social environment of the road is wildly unlike the rules of home. On the road, the rising rock stars wear their hedonistic appetites like badges of honor. That's why budding star Russell is thrilled by the promiscuous ardor of groupie Penny. But when the tour nears its end and Russell faces a return to wife and family, his social environment changes. Penny is now an embarrassment who must be sold off and shunned.

What unspoken social restrictions does Bill Murray face when he enlists in the U.S. Army of *Stripes*? How does the daily reality of *The Shawshank Redemption* differ from hero Andy's previous environment? Olive's performance during the *Little Miss Sunshine* contest is hilarious because it defies all sorts of social expectations. What are those expectations and what taboos does Olive challenge? The journalist hero of Clint Eastwood's *Midnight in the Garden of Good and Evil* claims that the Georgia society he's visiting is "like *Gone with the Wind* on mescaline." What social details bring him to that conclusion?

Let's take a look at *Legally Blonde* to see what the beginnings of our "social environment" essay might look like. The opening is set on the campus of a Southern California college where social functions are as important as academic events. Elle Woods is at the top of this food chain. She's wealthy, beautiful, and savvy, much admired by her sorority sisters and a top student in fashion marketing.

But the love of her life is moving on. Warner's family expects him to be a Senator from back East. In short, he needs to marry a Jackie, not a Marilyn. Elle's social environment can't understand this thinking: "Because I'm not a Vanderbilt, suddenly I'm white trash? I grew up in Bel Air, Warner. Across the street from Aaron Spelling. I think most people would agree that's a lot better than some stinky old Vanderbilt."

Elle could give Warner up, but she's heroic in her devotion. If she must be a Harvard law student to win her true love, then that's just what she'll do.

So let's examine the unspoken taboos she's challenging. Her application video befuddles the Harvard admission authorities, but (despite their East Coast social conditioning) they must acknowledge that she's done the hard work of passing their LSATs. She wins her spot in law school.

Elle learns that merely showing up in Massachusetts won't complete her mission. California and Elle's fashion world are about image and façade. The new universe of Harvard deals in substance, and displaced "fish" Elle must do more than dress the part to succeed here. The law school social environment is a dog-eat-dog competition. Students unprepared for combat face constant humiliation. Social butterfly blondes were valued back home. At Harvard, they are the butt of the joke.

What do we know about Harvard? About Massachusetts? About the East Coast? What are the origins of these places, and how did they get to be what they currently are? The writers picked this setting as a shorthand tactic to communicate lots of social custom information to the audience. Do consider specific references from the script, but don't pass up the opportunity to contemplate the implied details.

What is valued in this new place? How about willingness to aggressively attack weak-thinking classmates? Or a pecking order that esteems members of the "old money" class? Certainly, dedication to hard study is key. Can "nouveau riche" Elle become dedicated and willing while still retaining her West Coast social charms? Isn't that a significant dramatic question in this script?

This is a good start. But questions are better than answers in this exercise, and we can mine even more valuable information if we keep scanning the social environment.

What is the sexual environment here? A quick glance suggests that Harvard is sexless. But if we look again, we can find story gold beneath the surface. Sexually confident Elle rescues classmate Dorky David (a bratty girl is demeaning him) by publicizing him as a sexy love-'em-and-leave-'em stud. Elle and salon gal-pal Paulette get a lot sexier once they douse Paulette's loutish ex with a healthy dose of aggression. There is a catfight going on between Elle and Vivian, and even Professor Stromwell's initial nastiness towards Elle seems to have a sexual charge. These details don't even begin to explore the overt sex-and-career connection that Professor Callahan proposes to Elle.

Getting the idea? Then keep at it. Pore over the script to consider the social environment of all the characters, even the smallest, because who knows where the writer has hidden the juiciest information? As with all the Environmental Facts essays, the idea is to brainstorm and to keep the questions flowing.

Question the unspoken social attitudes of any story. How does the society being dramatized feel about homosexuality, capitalism, marriage, money, children, old people, ethnic minorities, communism, political elections, education? What class system is in operation? Are people highly regarded for their religious faith or are they mocked?

What "blind spots" are created because of the social environment?

THINGS TO THINK ABOUT

1. It delights social upstart Henry Higgins in *My Fair Lady* to pass off a guttersnipe like Eliza as a socially accepted lady. What taboos is he breaking?

2. Soldier John Dunbar of *Dances with Wolves* must earn his way into a different social order if he is to communicate with his Lakota neighbors. What is the social environment of his previous military world, and how does it change once he's alone on the prairie with the Sioux?

3. Bill Murray and Scarlett Johansson will be *Lost in Translation* for as long as they stay in Japan. To what social environments are they reacting, and what social mores of Japan are they missing?

NOTE FROM VOGLER

Here I go again, looking for meaning in the roots of words, in this case "social" and "society." They come from the Latin word "socius," which means companion, ally, comrade or partner, but was also a formal title granted to nations that were allied with Rome. The idea behind the word has something to do with shared interests that create binding connections. We speak of having "social ties" and of a "social contract," elements that bind us into a network of obligations and relationships. It pays to be aware, as a writer, of the social alliances that surround our characters and attempt to control their behavior.

Stories often begin with a breach in the social contract (murder, theft, cheating, war) or a strain in social ties (a misunderstanding, an insult, a betrayal). Or it may be that the hero suffers from a lack of social ties and the story is urging him or her to create some. That's one of the ideas at work in *Up in the Air*, where a man has worked very hard to live without any deep social connections and yet finds himself wishing for them. An essential element of some hero stories is that the hero grows into a social role — at first thinking only of himself but then taking greater responsibility and perhaps sacrificing himself to serve the greater needs of society.

CHAPTER NINETEEN

ENVIRONMENTAL FACTS 4: RELIGIOUS ENVIRONMENT

——— McKENNA ———

Religious Environment. It's an area prone to pat answers or to no answers at all. I mean, how many movies actually talk in religious terms? Sure, there's *The Exorcist* and *The Da Vinci Code*. But what's the religious environment in *Lethal Weapon* or *Something's Gotta Give*? Surely we can breeze over this chapter and move on. Right?

Let's not. And I say that because the fact that writers frequently leave religion unstated gives us a wide territory for introspection, exploration, and discovery. We are all plunked into life without a guidebook, and we spend much of our time here seeking reasons and meaning. We yearn to communicate with something larger than ourselves.

That search for meaning and communication builds an environment that subtly and deeply affects our characters. More importantly for us storytellers, the search can lead us to the all-important "question that must be asked."

Let's start with the obvious. On one level, the religious environment deals with an individual's relationship to gods, spirituality, and moral behavior. On this level, people are Methodists or Shiite Muslims. They may seek specified moral dictates propagated by a hierarchy of priests and religious authorities. Others may seek answers in Transcendental Meditation or mind-expanding drugs. The yearning may prod us to pray to an unseen force to grant our deeply felt wishes or to fulfill our fervent needs. Or it may inspire us to behave in ways that can't be explained by mere logic. The religious environment can inform us about the tactics people will and won't employ as they try to fulfill their "wants."

So to whom are we calling, and what do we seek? Take a look at your story and see how the characters communicate with their highest and most sacred forms of existence.

Here are two examples:

The title character in the two *The Thomas Crown Affair* movies executes elaborate robberies and places ridiculous sporting bets. *Million Dollar Baby* prizefighter Maggie pursues reluctant trainer Frankie beyond all reason.

Is there "story gravy" to be had in exploring these actions from a religious standpoint? We see Thomas Crown impulsively bet a fortune on his ability to complete a preposterous golf shot. Is he betting that his "gods" are favoring him? As for the robberies, we know from the outset that he's fabulously wealthy. If profit isn't his motivation, might it be that he's inspired the same way an artist is? Is he exploring his own personal religion?

We discover in *Million Dollar Baby* that both Maggie and Frankie are badly estranged from their families. Frankie attends daily Mass to question his isolation. The actions of both characters are prayers to find home, family, connection. Can we explore these ideas further in our religious environment investigation?

So far, so good. But there are other angles to this. For instance, can we profit by considering the religious aspects of a character who simply aspires to live in harmony with Creation? If we step in this direction, we may find complex religious environments in very unlikely stories.

For instance, writer-director "Bloody Sam" Peckinpah is usually cited for his exercises in ultra-violent machismo. But many of his movies are barely disguised meditations on morality. The religious environment may be the most important point within them. Peckinpah's *Ride the High Country* is a perfect example.

Here's the story in brief. Back in the day, legendary lawmen Judd and Gil tamed the frontier. But progress has reduced them to being errand boys for new big businesses. Gil sees no reason not to steal a corporate shipment of gold he and Judd have been hired to protect. But Judd answers to a higher principle, or as he puts it: "All I want is to enter my house justified." The battle between these two old friends is a religious parable.

Scriptural references and talk of morality (*Ride the High Country* is filled with both) provide obvious clues to the religious environment. But let's not limit our exploration. Let's keep probing. What happens if we take yet another angle to ask about characters' and society's highest aspiration?

Put another way, what is the "god" of this story?

There is little Scripture in Peckinpah's masterpiece, *The Wild Bunch.* But beneath all the gunfire and bloodshed, the story is steeped in matters of ethics and morality. Pike Bishop and his outlaw band are being pushed out of the new, corporate West. Hard times are undermining their outlaw code, and Pike must resort to deadly threats to keep his men in line.

"We're gonna stick together, just like it used to be! When you side with a man, you stay with him! And if you can't do that, you're like some animal, you're finished! We're finished! All of us!"

The Wild Bunch *heroes are armed for battle, but it's a showdown that puts their souls and their last chance for redemption at stake.*

Death haunts these men ("We've got to start thinking beyond our guns. Those days are closin' fast!"), and the Bunch yearns for an honorable exit. The script relentlessly places moral dilemmas about friendship, honor, and responsibility in their path. Under the trappings of a Western, Peckinpah creates a religious experience: a quest for redemption. The story becomes a purgatorial gauntlet from which the heroes and we ultimately emerge with cleansed souls. We find our honor and end the story in contact with our highest moral aspirations.

These examples are all fuel to fire your examination of the religious environment. The stories may not deal with churches, temples or mosques, but they do pose questions about day-to-day morality, something that speaks to the souls of all audience members.

To what "gods" are your characters responding? What is their highest aspiration?

We've been speaking about *Legally Blonde*, and it would be easy to ignore Elle's religious nature. But a second glance exposes that Elle is driven at all points by her sense of morality and decency.

She defends salon gal Paulette against an abusive ex-boyfriend even though Elle's classmates at Harvard would dismiss Paulette as white trash. That nasty Freshman Girl humiliates Dorky David in public until Elle's improvised flare-up ("I've already spent too many hours crying over you") recasts David as a cavalier stud. Surely these moments play into the story's religious environment.

But there's more to Elle than mere kindness. Beleaguered sorority sister Brooke entrusts her dark secret alibi to Elle, and Elle is under great pressure to break that trust. ("If you tell him, you'll probably make summer associate. Who cares about Brooke? Think about yourself.") But Elle's word is more important than approval from her teachers, employers and Warner. Religion rules over expediency for Elle.

It is moral decisions like this that draw us to Elle and have us root for her. However unlikely it may seem, religious values are the key to Elle's character and to the story.

What other values exist in this religious environment? Well, big-time professor and lawyer Callahan proves to be responding only to the gods of fame and power. We shun him when he fails to see Elle's decency of spirit and only desires her as a sex object.

We dislike Professor Stromwell when she makes Elle cry during that first class session, but she's redeemed in our eyes when she tells disheartened Elle: "If you're going to let one stupid prick ruin your life... you're not the girl I thought you were." In religious terms, Stromwell becomes the "good angel" encouraging Elle to combat the "bad."

Elle becomes a moral bellwether for us. Characters that can see her religious purity, like Vivian and Paulette, are our heroes. Characters like Warner never get it, and we enjoy their downfalls.

Screenwriters Lutz and Smith don't spend a minute talking about religion, but the religious environment of their story is specific and very detailed.

Before we wrap up here, let's consider a question I raised in the opening. What is the religious environment in *Lethal Weapon*? I'll start this journey by mentioning that Riggs wants to commit suicide and is thought to be a psycho. I'll also mention that his wife is recently dead. What can you make of that in religious terms? And what can you make of Jack Nicholson's appetite for thirty-year-old women and Diane Keaton's obsession with turtleneck sweaters in *Something's Gotta Give*? I bet all of these details connect to prayerful cries. What do you think?

THINGS TO THINK ABOUT

1. In John Huston's *The Treasure of the Sierra Madre*, the "god" of the story certainly appears to be the gold our three heroes are mining. But when newly wealthy prospector Howard insists that honor, gratitude, and duty demand the three heal the beneficent mountain they've wounded, even venal Fred C. Dobbs agrees to help. They are making a religious sacrifice.

   What other religious factors are at play in this script?

2. Religion becomes the focal point in Oliver Stone's work from the 1980s. In both *Wall Street* and *Platoon*, Stone posits actor Charlie Sheen as an Everyman pinned between religious polarities.

   In *Wall Street*, ambitious Sheen hungers for the wealth and power of ace corporate raider Gordon Gekko. To achieve it, he must embrace Gekko's amoral credo that "Greed is good."

   Sheen's working class father has higher hopes for his son, urging him to stop "going for the easy buck and start producing something with your life. Create, instead of living off the buying and selling of others." Which moral course will the young man choose?

   Which is the more important "god" of this religious environment? How does Stone play the two "gods" against each other in the script's individual scenes?

   Platoon drops Everyman Sheen in the ethical maelstrom of the Vietnam War. He's an unformed grunt, and like most grunts in the jungle, he's almost certain to be killed in combat. Who can save him?

   How should he behave? Well, Sgt. Elias is a good man who sees the radiant beauty of things. Sgt. Barnes is a ruthless killing machine. Barnes calls Elias a "crusader." Elias calls

Barnes a "prick." They're both right, and Sheen's character must decide which "god" he wants to serve.

Follow the step-by-step process by which Sheen's character draws his final conclusion.

3. What moral factors come into play for the heroine of *Sophie's Choice* when a Holocaust death camp officer promises to save one of her children if Sophie agrees to condemn her other child to death? What is the "god" in this situation?

NOTE FROM VOGLER

David and I have similar views on religion, seeing it very broadly as the things people believe in more than what church they go to, if any. As a young person I was a little cool to the shadowy world of film noir until David bolted me into a chair to watch an old movie called *Gilda* with him. Not only does it offer the sizzling presence of Rita Hayworth, but it also, according to the Book of David, deals in matters of cosmic import. He opened my eyes to an amazing sense that behind every little story of crime lords and petty gangsters there is a universe boiling with primal forces, an arena where God and the Devil are working out their eternal struggle, and sometimes it's hard to tell them apart.

It's fun to spot the hidden religious assumptions in movies that have no apparent connection to religion. If you start thinking this way, even *Pulp Fiction*, it turns out, can be read as an affirmation of the miraculous intervention of the divine in our lives.

CHAPTER TWENTY

ENVIRONMENTAL FACTS 5: POLITICAL ENVIRONMENT

——— McKENNA ———

Politics. Power. People. This should be fun.

We can agree at the beginning that stories set in the United States have an overt political environment of a democratic republic in which citizens vote for their executives and legislatures and respond to their judiciaries. All of this is completely true, but it's only the tip of the proverbial iceberg.

Let's search beyond the obvious. We are not looking for the single "right" answer. We are story detectives, scrutinizing and contemplating the small but telling details that will lead us to the "question that must be asked."

A storyteller may not specify the politics of a story any more than the religious environment, but every situation has political overtones. Students in a classroom taking notes from the lecturer who will grade them are in a political situation. Patients seeking treatment in a hospital emergency room or drivers trying to talk their way out of speeding tickets are also dealing with political realities that extend far beyond the core democratic republic.

In each of these instances, someone has power and someone else is seeking a response. That's an inherently political dynamic.

You know the term "office politics." What does it mean? Political power structures rule the workplace, regardless of whether that place is a global corporation or a mom-and-pop store in the neighborhood. Do "office politics" apply to your story?

Sports teams, street gangs and garden clubs all have political structures. There are even political power structures within friendships.

Who is in power, and how is that power assigned? Who wears the pants in a family and why? Does the power flow from top to bottom or the other way around? Is power won by fear, smarts, money, popularity, good looks, verbal wit? Does physical strength matter? Imagine stories and settings in which each one of these qualities is the deciding political factor.

Let's investigate from other angles. What do the people believe about the government that rules them? Are they idealistic supporters or are they skeptics? Is the government true to its word or are there "credibility gaps"? *Twelve Angry Men* deals with a jury's deliberations. The drama only occurs because the characters have varying degrees of faith in their political system.

What rights do individual citizens have in your narrative? What are their responsibilities? If we were living under the political conditions of your story, what could we expect our lives to be?

These are the sorts of questions that can further our political meditation. We might consider the explicit laws of our location and how these laws are made and enforced. Are they dictates from one person? Are they demands made from the grass roots? Do bribes, exchanged favors or political pork come into play? Who gets the final say? Can the laws be changed? If so, how?

Dig deeper. What mythic historical events shaped the foundation of the political system? Does it make a difference that our founding father is George Washington instead of Adolf Hitler?

What immediate historical events are affecting the moment we are dramatizing? Are we living in peace and prosperity or are we at war? If we are at war, who is the enemy and why are we fighting? If we are at peace, what is the group's political objective? Do we have a surplus of resources to be shared or is there a limited supply?

We can and should continue to unearth questions that open up new areas of political discovery. But let's take a breather and consider how one particular storyteller exploits the political environment and why.

Shakespeare has been celebrated for centuries for his poetry and understanding of individual human relationships. But I can't think of a writer more dedicated to the political environment tool. Just consider how often the instigating event in his plays is an act of political upheaval.

For instance, Prospero of *The Tempest* was a civic ruler who was deposed and exiled. The tragedy of King Lear deals with an attempt to transfer political power from one generation to the next. The King in *Hamlet* has apparently been assassinated. *Julius Caesar* occurs because one man has transformed a republic into a dictatorship. The essentially liberal Duke in *Measure for Measure* abandons his post and places fanatical judge Angelo in charge. Coriolanus is probably the best ruler that republican Romans could have, but he fails to win election because he metaphorically refuses to kiss babies.

Surrounded by his knife-wielding enemies, dictator Julius Caesar experiences radical regime change in this 1953 film version of the Shakespeare play. Few storytellers use the political Environmental Fact more effectively than William Shakespeare.

Shakespeare's political environment is important even when it isn't explicit and obvious. For instance, we'll miss much of the topsy-turvy humor of *A Midsummer Night's Dream* if we don't understand the usual political circumstances that the mischievous fairies are sabotaging.

Shakespeare knew that his audience had a deep-seated concern about political order. The history of his England had been marred for centuries by upheaval at the highest levels, and his current monarch had no heir to inherit the throne. Shakespeare bonded with his audience by intentionally and implicitly placing his stories in a political environment they all knew well.

That statement is true of almost all writers, so question the purpose of the story's power structure and political environment. Here are two examples that speak directly to the point:

Both examples were released as pop films in 1951, an era of Cold War fear and anxiety. In both, a mysterious alien arrives on Earth, and American forces battle to respond correctly. In both, the scientific community wants to protect the alien as a source of new knowledge while the military demands an armed response to what they see as a monstrous threat to mankind.

In *The Thing* (produced by Howard Hawks), the military priority of security proves to be the correct response. In Robert Wise's *The Day the Earth Stood Still*, that response would be disastrous, and the scientists' cry for acceptance and understanding wins the day.

At the core level, these two films are exactly the same except for the slightly different political environments. Surely this slight difference is essential to the storytellers' intentions. Don't these same political questions factor into more recent films like *Jurassic Park*, *Independence Day* and *District 9*? The nature of the political environment is as important as that.

The point is that there is an inherent political environment whenever two or more people interact. Knowing what it is and how it works can help us to create a reality that will resonate with our audience.

Back at *Legally Blonde*, the instigating event is notably political. The film begins with Elle preparing for her "perfect day" when Warner will propose to her. But instead of proposing, he dumps her. Why? Well, he has ambitions for a career in the U.S. Senate, and "If I'm going to be a politician, I need to marry a Jackie, not a — Marilyn."

The political environment influences Elle's status at Harvard. Classmates like Dorky David and militant feminista Enid earn immediate high status for their humanitarian work with Somali orphans and with Lesbians Against Drunk Driving. Elle doesn't notice (but we do) that her political accomplishments as Homecoming Queen and the president of Delta Gamma don't stack up.

Political sisterhood serves as the first basis of Vivian's bonding with Elle. ("Have you ever noticed that Callahan never asks Warner to bring him coffee? He's asked me at least a dozen times.") Both women have democratically earned their spot at Harvard while Warner's father "had to make a call," a pure political ploy. It seems that there's an "old-boy network" in order here. Say, does that suggest there may be value in considering who in the courtroom is male and who is female?

Politics also frames Elle's triumph as a lawyer because she and embattled client Brooke share a political history at Delta Gamma. Both are marginalized and disbelieved by power broker Professor Callahan, but Brooke knows she can trust Elle. When Brooke finds out that Elle is on her defense team, she breathes a sigh of relief: "Well, thank God one of you has a brain."

Is it fair to say that there are at last two political structures at play here? One of them metes out power on the basis of near-lethal competition, a harsh pecking order and winning at all costs. The other uses power cooperatively and relies on trust and the common good. Elle is dedicated to the latter, and it is the priority of this story. Could we make an equally effective story in which the other political structure is the appropriate priority?

THINGS TO THINK ABOUT

1. Martin Scorsese's *Casino* places two political environments in climactic conflict when the mob leaders of organized crime wrestle with the entrenched officials of Las Vegas. Do we ever determine which of the two environments wins out?

   The story also places the brains of the Robert De Niro character in direct conflict with the brawn of the Joe Pesci character. At various times, each character has political power. What factors determine when each character is the political top dog?

2. The politics of *Pulp Fiction* fixes Marcellus as an absolute ruler who must be obeyed (just ask Butch the boxer who was supposed to take a dive or Antwan who made the mistake of giving Marcellus' wife a foot massage). Can we speculate on the historical myth that began this power structure? Can we speculate on how Marcellus amassed his power?

3. The politics of *Slumdog Millionaire* insist that lowborn Jamal must be cheating to have the correct answers to a TV quiz show. What does this insistence say about the overall power structure? Can we speculate on the political priorities of that structure?

4. Key moments in the *Malcolm X* script written by Arnold Perl and Spike Lee define limitations imposed by the white political power structure on black citizens. Identify them. Also, identify and consider how the details of the black political structures in the script compare and contrast with the white power structure.

NOTE FROM VOGLER·

David and I both noticed, early on, that every world we came into contact with, be it a theatre company, a university administration, a military unit, a labor union or a movie studio, had a political component that had to be recognized and dealt with. You had to understand the forces at play, some obvious and above board, some subtle and almost invisible. Sooner or later you would have to choose sides in the see-saw struggle for power, just as characters in stories will have to do. You could try to stay neutral but that's almost impossible if you wish to be effective, as heroes in stories almost always find out.

You may find that some political awareness and savvy will come in handy as you try to sell your work or get it produced.

CHAPTER TWENTY-ONE

Environmental Facts 6: Economic Environment

——— McKENNA ———

The last "fact" we'll consider is the economic. As with the religious and political, there is an obvious level and an area that is subtler. We'll take a look at both.

On the obvious level, we're dealing with questions of economic class and relative wealth and poverty. In order to create drama, writers must invest their characters with a "want." Money is a common want, so it becomes a handy motivating factor for all sorts of storytellers. As Rod Tidwell from *Jerry Maguire* would have it: "Show me the money."

On this level, Patricia Highsmith's signature character Tom in *The Talented Mr. Ripley* covets his rich friend Dickie's status, and he murders him to steal it. The Coen Brothers' mad vision of *Fargo* gets going because cash-strapped car salesman Jerry needs loot to escape his wealthy father-in-law's tyranny. A simple theft of $40,000 leads lovelorn Marion Crane to *Psycho* Norman Bates' lair.

Maybe Tony Montana from *Scarface* expresses this simple level best of all: "In this country, you gotta make the money first. Then when you get the money, you get the power. Then when you get the power, then you get the women."

The dirty old man on the right has all the cash poverty-stricken Marion needs to buy her way into happiness in Psycho. *It's the instigating event for one of movie history's greatest plot reversals.*

There is more for us to discover on this level because the economic environment affects how people behave towards each other. How many 1930s screwball comedies rely on hare-brained heiresses who get paired with eager fellows from the lower classes? Jane Austen's enduring works are hip-deep in economic distinctions when her young would-be lovers ponder marriage.

In *Gilda* (1946), Johnny Farrell is a free spirit who sur-vives by chiseling small-time gamblers. But when he encounters powerful casino owner Ballin Mundson, he offers to become a servant. He wants to move up in economic class, and he endures the humiliation of being "hired help" to get there.

This situation is reversed in *It's a Wonderful Life* when George Bailey continually resists knuckling under to mean and miserly Mr. Potter's fortune: "You sit around here and you spin your little webs and you think the whole world revolves around you and your money. Well, it doesn't, Mr. Potter. In the whole vast configuration of things, I'd say you were nothing but a scurvy little spider."

We are taking a step forward with our economic environment questions when we consider who has the money and what the various characters will and won't do to get it.

DON'T SETTLE FOR EASY ANSWERS

Let's delve further.

For instance, in your story, does it matter how people make their money? When some characters are labor while others are management, the situation could easily detonate conflict and polarities. It's a divide that certainly fuels films like *Norma Rae* and John Sayles' *Matewan*.

Conflicts and polarities may arise because some characters are criminal while others are law-abiding or because some work for a salary while others enjoy trust funds. Investigate the source of the economy.

Do we discover useful conflicts and polarities by asking what people give up to earn a living? Working parents must give up time with their children. That has a clear dramatic effect on both the parents and kids in *Alice Doesn't Live Here Anymore, Kramer vs. Kramer,* and *The Pursuit of Happyness.* The effect is subtler but equally true in other stories. Cops, soldiers, firefighters, and other professionals risk their bodies. Innovators may have to sell their intellectual property in order to get by. How often must someone surrender personal dignity for the sake of survival?

Think of stories in which these economically-based polarities play a key role. Trying creating a story that is built on them.

FOLLOW THE MONEY

Let's back away and ponder another perspective. What is the original source of the economic power? A script may not specify details, but there is "story gravy" to be had in speculating on the source of Ballin's fortune (it becomes a subtle but important plot point) and how Mr. Potter became the richest man in town.

In George Stevens' *Giant*, newcomer Leslie creates a firestorm by suggesting that her moneyed in-laws and their fellow Texans stole their land from Mexico. Edward Albee's *Who's Afraid of Virginia Woolf?* makes a clear and telling point about marriage and progeny by specifying that almost all the money in the story is inherited from previous generations.

In each of these cases, the "original source" question substantiates and dramatizes how the world of our story works.

THERE'S ALWAYS ANOTHER WAY

We are still only scratching the surface. All the examples we've discussed so far take a capitalistic (money-based) economic system for granted. Could there be other economic systems at play?

What other sorts of economies exist? How about barter systems in which a person trades goods and services for other goods and services? How about communist idealists who seek a classless, stateless, oppression-free society of shared property? How about systems in which the concept of property doesn't even exist?

The Gods Must Be Crazy exemplifies that last idea. A remote tribe from the Kalahari Desert has no sense of personal property. When a wandering tribesman stumbles upon a Coke bottle that was thrown from a passing airplane, his neighbors believe it to be a one-of-a-kind gift from the gods. Civil unrest ignites when the ordinarily peaceful neighbors fight over this irreplaceable object. The tribesman's ensuing quest to return the gift to the gods sets off the comic adventure.

OTHER FORMS OF CURRENCY

I hesitate to leave the "obvious" level of the economic environment essay. There is more ground to till there. But I mentioned that there is a subtler level, too, and I want to get to it. It's this: must the notion of the Economic Environment pertain only to money? Can there be a different sort of "coin of the realm" in the universe of our story?

In Sergio Leone's *Dollars* trilogy, the characters seem driven by loot. But the loot doesn't ultimately have much effect. No matter how much gold Clint Eastwood amasses by the end of each film, he begins the next one wearing the same poncho and carrying the same few belongings. No, Leone's stories may claim to be about dollars, but the coin of his economic realm has to do with impossible sharpshooting and amoral survival skills.

Isn't that also true of the "made-men" of *Goodfellas*? On the surface, they are seeking the financial good life, but the core of their universe revolves around a peculiar notion of "respect." Offering or denying that "respect" is at least as important to the interactions of this piece as money.

Information and knowledge can surely be a coin of the realm. Hannibal the Cannibal in *Silence of the Lambs* barely owns the few items in his madhouse cell. But he has knowledge about an ongoing crime wave that forces heroine Clarice and her FBI mentor Jack to negotiate with him. The little hero of *The Sixth Sense* withstands his worst nightmare in the hope that the ghostly psychiatrist who haunts him knows how to make the other dead people go away.

This "coin of the realm" idea is a subtle element in the economic environment investigation. But it can lead to unexpected discovery. It's worth considering.

What are the economic factors in *Legally Blonde*? On the surface, it doesn't seem to matter because almost all the major characters appear well-to-do. Elle's lives in a mansion. Warner's family has enough money to send generations of its members to the U.S. Senate. All of the student characters can apparently afford the hefty tuition fees at Harvard Law School.

But let's continue to scout the economic landscape. For instance, when Warner rejects Elle because he needs a "Jackie" instead of a "Marilyn," the script makes a fine distinction between "old money" and the nouveau riche. One piece of evidence against accused murderess Brooke is that she may have married a much older man for his fortune. Even Elle makes this distinction by claiming that living across the street from Aaron Spelling is a lot better than associating with "some stinky old Vanderbilt."

"Old money" versus the nouveau riche is a recurring polarity in this story. Paulette and the delivery guy are laborers, a fact which also enters the equation.

Is there another "coin of the realm" in this story? At the risk of stretching the point, I suggest that Elle's loyalty and kindness complete "business deals" with Paulette, Vivian, Emmett, and Professor Stromwell that otherwise wouldn't happen.

We'll do well to note them in our economic essay.

THINGS TO THINK ABOUT

1. *Jerry Maguire* begins with a hero who questions the value of his high-paid work. As we've noted, Rod Tidwell equates money with love and respect. What other economic factors play out within this story? What are the economic polarities of this story and how are they resolved?

2. Now that we're considering Tom Cruise movies, what role do economic factors play in the hero's journey of *Risky Business*?

3. Think of a story about would-be lovers (say, *Romeo and Juliet*) and give each of them different economic backgrounds. How might this difference heighten the drama?

NOTE FROM VOGLER

David's on the money (sorry, I couldn't resist) in saying there is more than money at play in the economic dimension of some stories. There are other forms of currency and ways of measuring value. Economics (from Greek words that suggest management of a household) can also mean how you allocate and distribute resources such as time, energy and attention. It's been said that screenplays must be economical and that's true — you only have so much time and energy, and the audience has a limited amount of attention, so you must marshal these elements wisely.

CHAPTER TWENTY-TWO

ENVIRONMENTAL FACT: CONCLUSION

——— McKENNA ———

We've walked through the Environmental Facts. As scriptwriters, we've imbedded environmental clues to guide our artistic collaborators into the special three-dimensional world we originally imagined. As interpretive artists, we've pinpointed the clues the writer left for us. We've considered our story from angles that range from the overt physicality of Location and Date to the subtler qualities of Religion and Social factors.

So now let's compare our various essays to peg recurring themes and elements. If an element appears more than once, it's noteworthy and probably travels to the core of the special world the storyteller is creating.

We've examined *Legally Blonde* in six essays. What elements continually appear? What is the nature of that story? Take a look at what you've written and see what keeps popping up.

FISH OUT OF WATER

My essays reveal this as a "fish-out-of water" story. The location essay outlines Elle's journey from her natural Southern California habitat to a new world at Harvard Law School. The social, political, economic and religious differences between those two places cite specific and conflicting polarities I can exploit.

THE ARC OF THE JOURNEY

I explore these polarities in search of a workable theme. The characters all seem to exist on a spectrum between Acceptance and

Denial. Some are locked into a pattern of denial. Others are more accepting. Can this lead me to storytelling gold?

Let's consider Elle's emotional and intellectual journey. Beginnings are important, so where does she begin? In Elle's first scenes, she is preparing for her marriage proposal. Above all things she must look perfect for this night. Appearances are everything.

What is different at the end? By this time, Elle's worldview has expanded. Appearances still matter, but so does hard work and substance. She has found value in people like Vivian whom she had once despised. She has earned respect from Professor Stromwell and love with Emmett. All of these characters have learned to accept and have emerged fulfilled and victorious. Characters like Warner and Professor Callahan are stuck in denial and are doomed to defeat and failure.

MAKING DEDUCTIONS TO GET TO THE CORE

We're getting closer, but we're still not at the core of this. One detail that keeps popping up in the essays is the matter of preconceptions. Is this a story about prejudice? Can I support that opinion with the Environmental Facts I've detected?

Certainly Warner makes a prejudgment about the difference between the qualities of a girlfriend and those of a wife. Elle's guidance counselor and the enrollment committee at the law school have biases about who should and should not be admitted to Harvard. Elle's parents are stuck in the belief that Harvard people are serious and boring, very much unlike Elle's exciting success in beauty contests.

Even Elle has prejudices about stinky old Vanderbilts. I think we're onto something.

The story encourages us audience members to consider our own prejudices. I've laughed at dumb blonde jokes, so the story prompts me (and the audience) to look at the blonde stereotype with fresh eyes. That's a task I must keep in mind when I'm directing the story.

The writers toy with the stereotype from the very beginning. The sorority house of the opening sequence is filled with cheerleaders and party girls, a bouncy assembly line of bimbos. The dress shop saleswoman sees Elle as only a "dumb blonde with daddy's plastic."

Elle proves that she's got more substance than that, but even Elle falls prey to the stereotype. Her preparation for "the date" is all about her looks. The extent of her introspection only involves questioning whether her boobs are too big. She applies to Harvard with a bikini-clad personal statement and attends a law school party in a Playboy Bunny costume.

The stereotype urges me to see blondes as dumb, shallow, voluptuous, and utterly compliant. They are literally the butt of the joke. The writers also want me to experience positive blonde values. Elle may be soft-edged, but she has a soft heart that sees her defend oppressed characters like Paulette and Dorky David.

Elle is physically attractive and flirty, and these qualities give her the confidence to defy conventions. Convention-bound bigot Callahan is mystified by Elle's pink, perfumed resume. Open-minded Emmett travels beyond prejudice and accepts that the resume smells nice.

As a member of a beleaguered underclass, Elle sticks up for her oppressed sisters. She could advance herself by betraying Brooke, but she refuses to serve the prejudiced masters and aligns herself with her fellow blondes.

Unlike her small-minded foes who insist that competition is the prevailing order, Elle is generous with herself. She knows that blondeness is a state of mind, so she shares blonde secrets like the bend-and-snap with romance-challenged Paulette.

We're getting closer still. But we're not there yet.

WHAT IS THE TURNING POINT?

We know where Elle begins and where she ends. We're deducing themes of prejudice and a spectrum of Acceptance and Denial. Can we locate the moment when all of this comes together and reaches a climax? What moment marks the biggest change in the hero on her journey?

It seems clear that the turning point occurs when Elle is so defeated by prejudice (i.e., Callahan's sleazy seduction and Vivian's frosty response to it) that she decides to end her quest. "No more trying to be something I'm not." She's deaf to Emmett's response: "What if you're trying to be something you are?"

Now the script exposes the depth of the prejudice and its corrosive effects:

"No one's ever going to take me seriously. The people at law school don't, Warner doesn't — I don't even think my parents take me seriously. They wanted me to grow up and become a Victoria's Secret model who marries a rock star. Now, for the first time, it seemed like someone expected me to do something better with my life than wear underwear for a living. But I was kidding myself — Callahan didn't see me as a lawyer. He saw me as a piece of ass. Just like everyone else. It turns out, I am a joke."

Elle is finished, but she returns to her quest on the turning point of Professor Stromwell's response:

"If you let one stupid prick ruin your life, you're not the girl I thought you were."

Eureka! We've gotten to the core question! Who is Elle? What do we think of her? More importantly, what does she think of herself? Until this moment, she has been conceding to the world of anti-blonde prejudice. She has been seeking acceptance from others and living by their preconceptions of her. She's wanted Warner to pick her as his wife. She's wooed her law school classmates with costumes and food. She's yearned for Callahan to accept her. She's been victimizing herself.

From this moment forward, she follows her own star. She accepts responsibility for herself and the job at hand. Emmett and Stromwell help her up, but she conducts her devastating cross-examination on her own and contradicts Stromwell's axiom that "The law is reason free from passion."

This is the turning point that links the beginning polarity of Elle's journey to the end. Because I understand this structure, I can enter the special three-dimensional world that inspired the writers, and I can accurately dramatize the pieces of that world when I stage the script.

I see now that *Legally Blonde* enjoys a satisfying and cohesive narrative because the Acceptance and Denial polarities actively function in almost every moment of this story. Having identified these primary polarities, the writers smartly situated their heroine in a series of clear environments that make the most of them.

A cursory glance at *Legally Blonde* might cause the uninitiated to dismiss it as only an air-headed comic romp. Now that I am initiated, I know there's more to it than that. The feather-brained comedy is the wrapping. It's a vitally important component of the project. But the core of prejudice and self-acceptance is what makes the story smart and significant.

These are the deductions I make from my investigation. Surely, your essays include aspects I haven't considered. What elements have you unearthed and where do they lead you?

THINGS TO THINK ABOUT

Now that we have mastered the Environmental Facts, can we build a story from them? Arbitrarily select a Location and Date. Follow that by adding a character who has a "want." Then use the Religious, Social, Economic, and Political Environments of the Location and Date to construct obstacles the hero must face.

Once you've done this, use the Twelve Stages of a story that Chris has frequently outlined to shape an order of dramatic events and to build from the hero's Ordinary World through a Threshold Crossing and Supreme Ordeal to a climactic Resurrection showdown and a Return with an Elixir. Don't forget the Turning Point.

You have the tools at your disposal. Now implement them and work your way towards storytelling mastery.

NOTE FROM VOGLER

Way to go, David. As I look back at this multi-faceted way of looking at stories and characters I am reminded of the beautiful forms taken by natural crystals whose facets are intricately connected into coherent designs. I believe you'll find that if you actually do this exercise, it will crystallize your thinking! It's a wonderful feeling when that happens, when you feel you really understand the story on its many levels. It sort of snaps into clear focus and becomes almost a living thing. You can see not only the different levels, but how they are all connected to one another, creating a living network of relationships and conflicting forces.

CHAPTER TWENTY-THREE

What I Learned from Vaudeville

VOGLER

Back in the days before movies, radio and television, entertainment was provided by vaudeville, a circuit of theatres all over the U.S. and Canada that presented variety shows featuring all kinds of performers: singers, dancers, jugglers, animal acts, magicians, serious actors, and comedians. To arrange these unrelated acts into a coherent evening of entertainment, theatre managers developed a skill called "routining a show," that is, lining up the acts in a particular order to create a satisfying experience for the audience. Vaudeville has mostly vanished from the scene but it still has plenty to teach us about playing the emotions and expectations of the audience. In this chapter we'll look at how a manager routined a show and see if there's anything we can learn about constructing a good afternoon or evening of entertainment.

> Oh what a hit we made,
> We came on next to closing,
> Best on the bill, lovers until
> Love left the masquerade.

"Charade," lyrics by Johnny Mercer

It was these few lines from the title song of the movie *Charade* (1963) that led me to another source of story treasure, the forgotten know-how of vaudeville. I was puzzled by those phrases, "next to closing" and "best on the bill." Why was it important that "we came on next to closing"? And why was that the best thing on the bill? What bill? The song gave a few hints that the lovers it mentioned were performing some kind of masquerade or charade on a stage, for there are references to "darkened wings" where a "music box played on," but the full meaning of those phrases eluded me.

When I started acting in local theatre productions in San Antonio I asked some of the more experienced actors about the song. One veteran thespian told me exactly what was meant by "best on the bill" and "next to closing." These, he said, were terms from the grand old tradition of vaudeville.

The "bill" was the playbill that was printed up daily to be posted in front of the theatre, a kind of menu of the evening's entertainment, listed in the order the acts would be presented. The best "billing" in an evening of vaudeville amusement, the best position from the performer's point of view, was not the last place, but the next to last place. One might think, as I did, that the last place was the most important because that would give the show its big finish and send the audience out happy. Surely they would save the biggest and best act until last?

But in fact, my acting mentor told me, the most desirable place is *just before* the last act, because this is the real climax of the evening. The next-to-last act brings the audience to a high point of emotion and sensation, a sublime moment of plea-sure or an explosion of laughter. The final act has a different purpose. It must be loud and lively to overwhelm the noise and distraction of people getting ready to leave the theatre. For the star or "headliner," next-to-closing was the sweet spot on the bill, where the audience had been brought to the perfect pitch of excitement, ready to be knocked over by a strong perfor-mance. After doing some encores and taking a few extra bows, the headliner left the stage while the audience was still thrilled, and the band struck up for the noisy final act, a patriotic song or a sing-along to a popular tune that sent the audience away satisfied.

Later, when I started writing and critiquing screenplays, I realized the "next to closing" spot had its parallel in screenwriting. The most important moment in a script was usually not the very last scene, but the scene before last, where the tension was at its highest point and the hero risked everything on one throw of the dice. I began looking for other clues from vaudeville and eventually discovered that the techniques for arranging a satisfying evening of entertainment were called "routing the show."

ROLE OF THE MANAGER

In the early days of vaudeville, figuring out the routine for an evening and drawing up the bill was the province of the local theatre manager, a master of many skills. Later, when vaudeville became a huge industry with thousands of performers run from syndicates in the big cities, the routing was done by the central office, but the local theatre manager still had a lot of authority to make on-the-spot decisions. Acts scheduled by the central office in Manhattan might miss trains, be held over in Duluth or show up drunk in Des Moines, and the man on the scene had to make the final calls about what went up on his stage.

THE SHOW MUST GO ON

The local theatre manager often had to decide the shape of the evening's program based on what acts got off the train that day. Vaudeville in America and Canada was made possible by the railroad system, and performers were constantly traveling to provide fresh entertainment to thousands of vaudeville palaces in every city in North America. If the dancing mules were delayed or the star soprano missed her train, the manager had to put together some kind of entertainment, by the ancient rule of the theatre: The Show Must Go On! This might mean going out into the street to find some kid to do bicycle tricks, or looking for new local talent by holding open auditions, or asking the performers who did show up to dust off an old act or put something together on the fly. One way or another, the manager had to put on a show. The comedy team of George Burns and Gracie Allen gained a reputation as a reliable "disappointment" act that could be thrown in when a much-anticipated act was unable to perform, and many stars got their first big break when they filled in so the show could go on.

The theatre managers were masters of the fine old art of showmanship, a set of skills all but forgotten by the current generation of entertainers. The manager was a hard-headed businessman, a shrewd psychologist, and a backstage mechanic, but he was also an artist. His canvas was the stage and his brushes and oils were the acts he presented, sequenced so as to create maximum emotional effect. He arranged them in a logical progression, following definite principles of entertainment design, distilled from centuries of theatrical experience.

THE PRINCIPLE OF CONTRAST

The first and most important design principle considered by the manager was alternation or contrast. Vaudeville was conceived as an evening of "variety," presenting a pleasing menu of different kinds of entertainment, something for every taste. It seemed to work best when the acts were as different from one another as possible, providing the maximum in contrast and variety. As artists have discovered the world over, contrast heightens any artistic effect. Silence can be felt more deeply when contrasted with noise; colors seem more vibrant when put against their opposites on the color wheel, blue against orange, red against green, yellow against purple. In painting and in stage design, the eye is drawn to the area with the most contrast.

This meant that the manager would plan on constantly varying the type and emotional tone of the acts throughout the evening. A noisy, frenetic act like a knockabout comedy skit would be followed by a single performer singing a ballad or a sentimental song. Serious and funny, fast and slow, big and little, musical acts and short plays, broad physical comedy and witty verbal humor, all these qualities and styles would be contrasted in the course of the show.

There was a practical reason for one aspect of this principle of contrast, the alternating of "acts in one" which were solo or duet performances, down in front of the main curtain, right by the footlights, and "full stage acts" that took up the whole performance space with sometimes elaborate sets and dozens of people and animals leaping about the stage. Closing the curtain and featuring the small-scale act left time for the stagehands to move backdrops, furniture and props for the big act to follow. The alternating of the full stage acts and the "acts in one" created the equivalent of cinema's long shot and close up, changing the scale of the performances back and forth to give visual variety.

DISNEY AND CONTRAST

Walt Disney was a keen student of vaudeville, and once shocked his father by appearing onstage in a balancing act in a Kansas City theatre. He thoroughly embraced the cadences and traditions of vaudeville, especially this principle of contrast, and applied them faithfully to his animated cartoons and, later, live action movies. You can see the idea at work in any Disney movie, where fast-paced action sequences and wide vistas are contrasted with calmer and more intimate "getting to know you" scenes featuring big close-ups of the characters, the equivalent of the "acts in one." You can see it especially well in the structure of *Fantasia*. Its musical segments could have been a random collection, but a master entertainer has arranged them by the principle of contrast, alternating pieces that are fast and slow, serious and funny, all building on one another to create a satisfying emotional climax.

Application: We can use the principle of contrast in our storytelling today, making sure that our "acts," sequences or chapters don't get repetitive, that we don't have two chase scenes or two love scenes in a row, that we keep the audience's interest by constantly changing up the rhythms and pace of our show.

If a certain scene is not having its desired emotional effect, consider increasing the contrast with the previous scene to enhance the impact you are after.

Vivid contrasts and alternating between intensity and relaxation can act like a pump on the audience's emotions. Intensity applied without rest would soon tire an audience, but the alternation with periods of relative calm allows people to recover slightly before going on to enjoy higher levels of intensity.

PLACING THE HEADLINERS

Every vaudeville show needed a headliner, a well-known and currently popular star or act that could attract big crowds. That act would automatically be assigned the most desired and crucial place on the bill, next to closing. With this key piece in place, the manager could then begin to place the other acts available to him, ordering them with the aim of building the entire evening to support the specific emotional effect of the headliner's act.

If the headliner happened to be a big comedy star, the evening could take on a general tone of merriment, but with a tender, sentimental or serious moment here and there for contrast. Comedy was always the mainstay of vaudeville, but sometimes the headliner was a serious performer from the "legitimate" theatre, a tragic actress like Sarah Bernhardt performing highlights from Shakespeare, or a famous opera singer like Jenny Lind. Such a headliner required a different balance of acts, with a slightly more serious or classy tone, to prepare the audience for a more refined emotional effect at the climax of the evening.

However, just for contrast and for comic relief, the tone of high culture would likely be brought back down to earth by a raucous comedy finish, perhaps what was called a "dumb act," meaning an act not dependent on dialogue, perhaps one filled with physical gags. Buster Keaton broke into vaudeville as a child performer in such an act, being comically thrown around the stage by his father in what was known as a "knockabout" comedy, with little or no dialogue.

Application: Know what your climax will be and build your story structure accordingly. Every choice in the script or novel should be made with one eye on the climax, asking yourself, does this choice support that climax, does it lead inevitably but surprisingly to that highest point of tension or drama in your story? Does the general tone of the story support the big emotional effect you want to create in the next-to-last scene?

Charlie Chaplin, who served his apprenticeship in British music halls, the equivalent of American vaudeville, tried to structure his films so that audiences would either "Laugh a lot and cry a little," or "Cry a lot and laugh a little," meaning that the overall emotional weight of the story, whether serious or funny, has to be balanced properly by a smaller amount of a different feeling in order to create contrast and keep the main emotion from being overwhelming or tiresome. Dramas can be too heavy for their own good and need the leavening of comic relief, while comedies can be too frivolous and may need a bit of gravity, a touch of real danger or sadness, to give the comedy some bite.

FILLING OUT THE BILL

Having secured a headliner and determined the general direction of the evening, the manager could proceed to fill the blanks in the bill, but with definite purposes in mind for each position. A typical vaudeville show presented eight or nine acts with an intermission. The second part would usually be shorter than the first, so as not to tire out the audience waiting for the headliner to appear. Shorter programs without an intermission might be run three times a day, just as modern movie theatres screen their films several times a day. These shorter shows would have five or six acts but would follow the general rules of routining, minus the intermission.

The acts would be assigned as follows:

1. The **OPENING ACT** must be loud and lively, ideally with little or no dialogue. This is for the practical reason that many people are still finding their seats and settling in. In vaudeville this would be a "dumb act" such as jugglers, acrobats, clowns or performing animals, taking up the full stage. It's not high status from the performers' point of view, but it serves an important purpose.

   Application: Unless you are Ingmar Bergman, it's probably a good idea to start a story with something visual, establishing a location, specifying a world, introducing a character in action. This is the time for the long shot perspective. Save intense, close-up dialogue scenes for a few minutes into the narrative, after the audience has had time to get settled. Give them a moment to get oriented and learn something about the characters from observing their behavior and their world.

   In the beginning, you are trying to separate the audience from their day-to-day concerns, inviting them to step into the Ordinary World of your hero. In a way you are trying to enchant them or put them into a trance. You might need something dramatic, exciting or exotic to get them in the right frame of mind. Magician acts made a good opening for a vaudeville show, requiring little or no dialogue and establishing the tone of wonder.

2. **SECOND POSITION** is a step up in status, usually featuring an "act in one," one or two performers doing a song and dance act or a comedy skit in front of the curtain while the scenery is frantically being changed backstage. It should be more entertaining than the first act, in other words, it should "top" the act before it. Ideally this should be true of

each successive act in the show until the climax is reached, next-to-closing.

Application: "Always top yourself" is one of the oldest rules of vaudeville and all of show business. The audience should always be made to feel "That was amazing! It couldn't possibly get any better!" and then it does. Each joke or gag, each chase or fight scene, each tense emotional confrontation should be better than the last, building steadily towards the climax.

If a vaudeville performer returned to a theatre after making a sensation in that town a year ago, he knew audiences would expect him do their favorite bits again, but he also knew he was obligated to top himself with new material, better than last year's. Great careers are built on a succession of triumphs, each outdoing the ones before. There will be inevitable failures and less impressive efforts in any career, but the artist keeps trying to improve with the aim of giving the audience more pleasure.

The equivalent of the second position in many stories is a sequence where the audience gets oriented to the story, connecting emotionally to the hero's desires and learning what great forces are in play. The opening can be flashy but what comes after is probably more human and intimate to create contrast and allow the audience to plug themselves into the emotional currents of the story.

3. **THIRD POSITION** in a vaudeville show usually fills the stage, creating a whole world for the audience to be immersed in. It could be a comedy sketch set in a home or office, a big band and dancers performing several numbers, a condensed version of a Broadway play, or an elaborate circus act with trapezes, elephants, and zebras.

Application: Once a story has made the emotional connection between the hero and the audience, it's time to thrust them into a new world, onto a new stage. This corresponds to the Hero's Journey elements of Crossing the Threshold and entering the Special World.

4. **FOURTH POSITION** is important because it's usually the next to last act before the intermission, and it has to serve as the climax for the first half of the show. Often a second headliner, an important, popular singer or comedian, would be given this spot, considered just a little less desirable than next-to-closing. Sticking to the principle of alternation, this act would have a different feeling than the act before it, and was usually a small-scale, intimate "act-in-one." Such an act needed a strong finish that left the audience gasping, thrilled or convulsed with laughter.

   Application: A work of entertainment needs at least two climaxes: the next-to-final moment, of course, but also a secondary or lesser climax somewhere in the middle, or perhaps a little past the middle. This corresponds to the Ordeal phase of the Hero's Journey pattern. Fourth position is the climax of the first half of the show, surpassing everything that has come before, but it must not eclipse the final climax.

5. **FIFTH POSITION** was not as desirable as fourth, because people were impatient for the intermission and a bit more inattentive, but it had to be filled carefully with an act that ended the first half with a bang. It would usually be a stage-filling extravaganza, something upbeat that offered the audience a colorful treat before the intermission, or a surprising or sensational effect that gave them something to talk about while refreshing themselves. The intermission itself was important, giving the audience a chance to move around, discuss the evening so far, and gather energy to enjoy the rest of the performance.

Application: This can be matched to the Reward phase of the Hero's Journey, where the hero may celebrate his victory over death and fear. Reward scenes allow audience and characters to catch up a bit and take a breather before committing to the last act. They often involve a meal in which the characters take in energy and digest what has happened to them.

6. **SIXTH POSITION** was a curtain-raiser, vital to re-establishing the current of energy in the evening. Often an "act in one," it had to strike quickly to get the audience back in their seats and paying attention. It could be a musical soloist or a silent comedy act, but it had to have energy and speed. The pace of the evening had to quicken, to overcome the audience's tendency to get sleepy after eating or impatient to get home.

Application: In the Hero's Journey, The Road Back may be the beginning of the last act, and it shares the sixth position's need for velocity and renewed energy. That's why so many movies have chase scenes at this point, a tried and true method of reviving the audience's flagging attention with increased jeopardy, suspense and physical movement.

7. **SEVENTH POSITION** would typically return to the full stage for a big comedy sketch or condensation of a hit play. This act was meat and potatoes, a solid and satisfying main dish of entertainment, but still leaving room for the special treat of the act to follow.

Application: After a big chase scene or action scene in a movie, there may be a need for a meaty dramatic scene, bringing the inner journey of the hero to a high point that tops all the similar scenes that came before.

8. Finally we come to the most desirable position for a performer, **NEXT-TO-CLOSING**, the **eighth position** in

a nine-act show, with the privilege of top billing on the theatre marquee. This is what the audience was anticipating all evening, the true climax of the experience. Whatever it was, it needed to be sensational or sublime, topping everything and everyone on the stage thus far. It could be a show-stopping aria, a heart-breaking dramatic turn, or a hilarious comedy routine, but it absolutely had to top the previous acts, or the whole show would be a dismal failure. In a well-routined show, the act next to closing would somehow echo the emotions evoked in all the other acts, summing up the evening in one divine moment.

Application: Next-to-closing has the same weight and importance in any kind of story, the moment when you definitely top yourself with your best material, the finest moment for you and your character, the maximum height of tension and suspense, the biggest explosion of action or comedy. It should trigger a final, irresistible, cathartic release of all the emotions and tensions you have evoked in building up to this point. It can have the power to actually transform members of the audience, guiding them to a moment when they realize new possibilities for themselves.

9. **NINTH** (and final) **POSITION** was almost as undesirable as first position, because the audience already had the experience they came for, and were rustling around getting ready to bolt from the theatre. But the job was just as important as any other, for the show had to be finished properly, in a big way, with a lot of noise, color and spectacle, filling the whole stage with a final impression of lavish entertainment. Patriotic numbers and sing-alongs were effective, giving the audience a final feeling of community. Often the whole cast of the show would come out on the stage for a final bow. But it should be over quickly, allowing the audience to escape into the night while still in the magic bubble of entertainment.

Application: When the main work of the story has been done by the climax, the rule is: Get off the stage as soon as possible. But there may be time, and a need for, a denouement, a final piece that gives a coda or states the moral or resolves the final details of the plot. It might project a little into the future, suggesting the spreading ripple effect of the hero's courageous choice in the climax. It could be a little treat for the audience, almost like a souvenir from the journey, or it might show a vast vista for future exploration. But in any case you should not linger, and should clear the stage promptly so the magic bubble doesn't pop too soon.

PUTTING IT INTO PRACTICE

I got a chance to test what I had learned from vaudeville when I took a week-long workshop on improving vision. The workshop leader, a brilliant man named Peter Grunwald, was very creative about using games, exercises, and drills in our training, and one of his tricks was that after several days of work he suddenly announced we were going to put on a vaudeville show that evening. Between lunch and dinner we had to appoint someone as the master of ceremonies and put together an evening of variety entertainment, with each person showing some talent such as juggling, singing, dancing, playing an instrument, telling a little story, telling some jokes, putting on a skit, etc.

The group, knowing my show biz background, was unanimous in choosing me as the master of ceremonies, although I knew I was really stepping into the shoes of the vaudeville manager. Fortunately I had just been reading about vaudeville, and knew exactly what to do. All afternoon I went around asking people what talents they could display, looking for a logical and satisfying sequence to arrange them in.

Following the vaudeville laws of routining a show, I was looking for my headliner, my magical "next-to-closing" act. Before long I found an act that fit the bill, provided by someone with a background in running church camps who proposed singing a little song about seeing the spirit inside another person. The idea was for the singer to call up someone from the audience and sing the song to them, with hand gestures to indicate respect and acceptance of the divine in that person. The first singer then guided that person to select another audience member to come up and be included in a growing circle, singing the song and performing the gestures, and so on until the whole stage was filled and everyone was included in the circle. It had the right emotional potential to be a terrific climax for our evening of vaudeville.

The rest of the afternoon I spent in arranging the other acts around the vaudeville principle of contrast, making sure to follow comedy bits with more serious acts, and to alternate "acts in one" with full stage acts. I also tried to think about the overall tone of the evening, which would surely be to let them laugh a lot and cry a little. I arranged the acts to have a strong opening and then to build from there, always topping ourselves, with more laughter and emotional intensity piled on until the climax delivered its emotional punch.

It worked like a charm. After laughing ourselves silly for most of the evening, we were all deeply moved by the simple ritual of the religious camp song. We closed with a simple sing-along, led by one of the workshop participants, that gave the evening a perfect finish, and everybody went to bed happy, feeling well entertained and part of something.

That was a rare opportunity to produce my own vaudeville show, but I use the tools of vaudeville all the time in consulting on big-budget Hollywood movies.

Though many mourned the death of vaudeville, especially performers who had lived through its golden days, some say it never really died, it simply transformed itself into radio, movies, and TV shows. Either way, some of its life still breathes in our show business language and in our endless need to be amused with variety, artfully arranged to produce a satisfying evening of entertainment.

NOTE FROM McKENNA

This chapter and the next one on "Showmanship" make me nostalgic for my beginnings in this business. Growing up on televised movies, my hero was James Cagney in *Yankee Doodle Dandy*. It's the life story of a kid vaudevillian who becomes the biggest thing on Broadway. That's the life I was going to have.

I got my start as a theatre apprentice at the Playhouse on the Mall, a stock theatre run by Robert Ludlum. He was years away from becoming the best-selling author of the Bourne novels, and his boisterous enthusiasm for the biz made me feel that he'd been raised on the same dreams that were feeding me. Mel Brooks' film *The Producers* had just opened, and Bob re-named himself "Max Bialystock" in honor of that theatrical huckster.

Bob understood on the cellular level how to work his audience in order to survive. If the house was skimpy for a given performance, he'd sit in the back row to prime the laughter pump. He'd barge out of his office just before every act break so he could noisily generate curtain applause and "bravos" from the shadows. He was masterful at massaging egos, throwing well-timed hissy-fits and initiating underpaid kids into a world that looked tacky in its details but which became sublime under the magic of stage lighting.

Bob's big moneymaker at the Playhouse was an annual tour stop of Ann Corio's *This Was Burlesque*. A tall beauty, Ms. Corio had incensed New York's mayor Fiorello LaGuardia in the 1930s and enchanted a generation of Harvard under-graduates with her provocative dance numbers. She must have been astonishing in her day. By the time I met her, she was old enough to be my grandmother, so it astonished me that she had enough stage-savvy to perform a shimmering (and damned erotic) strip number in the next-to-closing position.

Her troupe included singers, showgirls, strippers (one of whom incorporated a talented python into her act), top bananas, stooges and straight-men. She even had a candy butcher who had the greatest come-on sales spiel I've ever heard. They were well-drilled in the vaudeville tradition, as disciplined in their backstage manner as they were madcap in front of the audience.

I was a green-as-grass sixteen-year-old kid in suburban New Jersey, but for a full month every year, Bob Ludlum and Ann Corio transported me into the universe of *Yankee Doodle Dandy*. What I saw and learned there had everything that Chris describes in his chapter.

In a hundred words or less, what I learned from vaudeville is that I and you (if you choose to accept this mission) are part of a tradition that arguably extends back to the origins of storytelling and performance. We are the story of mankind. I urge you to get hungry for knowledge of what has gone before you because that knowledge lights your path forward.

Showmanship

VOGLER

There's more in the steamer trunk of vaudeville lore, waiting to be revived and put to modern uses. The local theatre manager's skill of routing the show is part of something larger, the fine old art of Showmanship. This consisted not only in a sense for talent, timing and what would thrill an audience, but also in a host of other abilities including building relationships with the community. "Public Relations" or PR was an important part of vaudeville, meaning that the local manager learned the rhythms and tastes of his community and worked hard to make the theatre part of the region's culture. The theatre itself became a community resource, a place for hosting religious and patriotic events and meetings of local clubs.

Showmanship also meant creating anticipation and excitement for upcoming shows using every trick in the entertainer's book. If the manager had booked a circus act, he'd turn the unloading of the animals from the train into a festive event, and make a parade out of the transfer of the animals to the theatre. Important performers were welcomed at the station with literal fanfare from the theatre's orchestra. A drum of excitement was kept beating for weeks in advance of the arrival of a big star. All kinds of events were planned to create anticipation for a big headliner, such as look-alike contests and sing-alongs of that performer's signature tunes.

Much of vaudeville showmanship was adopted into the culture of the movies, and in the period after World War II great showmen like Cecil B. DeMille, Joseph E. Levine, and Samuel

Z. Arkoff promoted movies and stars in the grand tradition of vaudeville. If DeMille had an Egyptian-themed picture to sell, he'd make sure the local theatre had actors in Egyptian costume in the lobby and an Egyptian chariot parked outside, and for weeks before the movie opened local schools and church groups would be bombarded with "study guides" themed around the movie. The high school band would get sheet music of the movie's themes.

Levine bought up a cheesy Italian sword-and-sandal flick called *Hercules* and drummed it into a box office titan with hyperbolic advertising ("Mighty Saga of the World's Mightiest Man!") and promotional gimmicks, and later did the same with an obscure Japanese science fiction product, *Godzilla*. With a keen understanding of human nature he turned a weak Australian import into a smash hit simply by changing the title from *Walk into Paradise* to *Walk into Hell*.

Arkoff, who partnered with Roger Corman and James H. Nicholson to produce many memorable genre films and launch many acting and directing careers, once gave a formula for box office success based on the letters of his last name.

THE A.R.K.O.F.F. FORMULA

Action: Thrilling, compelling drama

Revolution: Novel, daring themes and subjects

Killing: A tasteful amount of violence

Oratory: Good dialogue or memorable speeches

Fantasy: Fulfillment of widely-held audience wishes or fantasies

Fornication: Something sexy, especially appealing to young adults

Like a well-routined vaudeville show, his formula provides plenty of contrast and has something for everyone.

Showmanship today can mean clever use of new technology, intelligent branding and marketing, but also all the old theatrical tricks for creating interest, anticipation, and desire to experience a new sensation. Sometimes in a technological world, the "brute force" techniques of the old showmen, such as doing stunts and spectacles in public places and working at the local level to create interest in a coming attraction, can awaken primal feelings that no amount of technology can stimulate.

Showmanship can be improvisational and opportunistic, taking advantage of even negative publicity to promote a production. The actor Burt Lancaster revealed his showmanship when he was stung by press criticism that he employed stunt doubles for the filming of his action picture *The Flame and the Arrow*. To counteract the critics, and draw attention to his production, he staged public demonstrations of high-risk circus stunts, performed with his co-star from the film and good friend, Nick Cravat. They had grown up in the circus together and their amazing public stunts turned a press problem into tons of free publicity for the movie.

Showmanship doesn't mean promoting shoddy material with overblown hype. The true showman is actually presenting something of value, a quality product, an immense spectacle, an intense drama, a hilarious comedy or a special talent that the public is eager to see. Stan Lee of Marvel Comics fame is a great showman who uses high-flying hyperbole and aggressive alliteration to promote his products, but his extravagant style is justified by the high quality of his output. He generates truly entertaining stories with realistic characters and vivid artwork and his style of promotion expresses his genuine enthusiasm for the product and the artists who created them.

SELL THE SIZZLE, NOT THE BACON

I had the honor of working with Mr. Lee once on a project, and will pass on a bit of showmanship that he revealed to me. I had been writing treatments for him on a Marvel property, treatments that he kept rejecting. I finally found out it was because they were too detailed and specific. "Sell the sizzle, not the bacon," Stan said, concisely describing an entire philosophy of pitching. He wanted something more general and more evocative, something that would not get bogged down in details, but that would create a certain feeling about the project, an impression of all the wonderful things it would deliver rather than a step-by-step outline of the plot. It was too easy for studio executives to pick apart a detailed story, Stan said, so he preferred to give them something that sizzled and smelled like a big hit, stimulating their senses without delivering the full meal. The art of pitching is another subject, but it's part of showmanship, for the showman needs to know how to enticingly describe the product to potential backers and audiences.

Showmanship has many dimensions, from creating the impression of local interest to harnessing the latest technology for promoting entertainment, and it will continue to evolve. Recently movie producers discovered the power of comic book conventions to launch new projects with showmanship tailored to the target audience.

SOMETHING TO THINK ABOUT

What creative use of showmanship was used to promote *Titanic*? *Avatar*?

What showmanship can you apply to marketing and promoting your own talents?

We all have a beloved film that didn't get the box office or critical attention that we think it deserved. How would you have used showmanship to promote that movie so it could reach its full potential?

CHAPTER TWENTY-FIVE

Five-Year Plan for Aspiring Professional Screenwriters

McKENNA

Let's cut to the chase. Most people read books like this one to learn how to make a killing (or at least a living) in the screen trade. So let's lay out a five-year attack plan that will increase your chances of having that dream come true.

A Five-Year Plan: Begin with the understanding that there is no such thing as overnight success. Fame and fortune may hit all at once, but they are almost always preceded by a long, arduous stretch of thankless hard work and dedication. If you aren't prepared to make a long-term commitment, you'd be wise to aim at a more accessible target.

A Low Maintenance Job-Job: You can get paid to write almost immediately. You accomplish this by finding a low-pressure job that provides an income. You can use that income to hire yourself to write. So, immediately, you are a professional writer.

What sort of job are you looking for? Your objective should be the most amount of money for the least amount of work. You are trading your time for cash. Your real job is to write.

So you probably don't want a gig that requires the greater part of your brain space. This eliminates a job-job as an astronaut, a Wall Street broker or a presidential candidate. Too much physical work and emotional commitment.

The best writer's job-job I've ever heard about comes from my friend Mark Fergus who co-wrote *Iron Man*. During his salad days, Mark signed on to be a night watchman. The job required that he be present in a quiet building for eight hours at a time. He needed to make the rounds for only a few minutes a night. During the rest of the time, he was plunked down in a chair with nothing to do but write. The job had absolutely no social status, but it gave him the time and the money to fund his writing career. After a few years, he left the job with cash in his pocket and a few spec screenplays in his portfolio. An ideal choice for an aspiring writer.

Work Every Day: Alfred Bester, one of the great hack writers of the pulp fiction era, claimed that he wrote every day because he was "reporting in." He disciplined himself to get into the writer's "trance" and to sort out his thoughts on the page.

Writers write. If you can't bring yourself to get your butt in the chair every day, then do consider that you are chasing an inappropriate dream.

What sorts of things might you write? Well, obviously I'd have you work on your scripts and screen stories. But I'd at least have you set aside several hours each day to write in a diary, to commit to personal correspondence (old-fashioned letters, not e-mails which are the equivalent of brain farts) and to work on a newspaper file (more about that in a minute).

Among other things, writing is a habit. If you can't get into the habit, you probably aren't a writer.

Newspaper Files: This involves a couple of things. The first is that you are actually reading a newspaper. I have nothing against reading news on the Internet, but I remind you that there's something magical about having an actual paper filled with written news reports in your hands.

When I suggest that you build a file, I'm not simply urging you to clip articles to be placed in a folder. That just creates trash that will clutter your workspace.

No, once you clip an article, write a few paragraphs about it. What about the article caught your interest? What is the essential drama in the story? Who are the leading characters?

What are their conflicts? What do they want and what obstacles stand in their way? How would you turn the article into a film?

Do this every day, and you'll develop habitual discipline that can channel your writing ambitions.

Read: Reading is the flip-side of writing, so get into the habit (there's that word again) of reading voraciously.

Read everything. If you are dedicated to horror stories, crack open a romance bodice-ripper now and again. If your area is kitchen sink domestic dramas, pick up an occasional spy thriller. There's no telling what you can learn by seeing how other writers in other genres ply their craft. Maybe they can turn you on to a trick you can apply to your specialty.

Read what sells. If you intend to become rich and famous in this business, you ought to familiarize yourself with what the audience is buying. Cultural snobs may disregard unpretentious writers like Dean Koontz, Jackie Collins, and James Patterson, but craftsmen like these are perpetually on the job and at the top of the best-seller lists. What do they know about connecting to an audience that you should be learning?

Read Something Good: Mark Twain famously said that a classic is a "book which people praise and don't read." I urge you to reverse that trend as part of your five-year plan.

About four times a year (once every season), I'd have you pick up a classic and find out what's in there. Read some Cervantes or Twain or Faulkner. You may have seen all those Jane Austen movies, but what does her work look like on the page?

A few years ago, I had a couple of weeks with little to do. I realized that I had never read Shakespeare's "problem plays." Like every other schoolboy, I had read the basics of *Hamlet*, *Othello*, and *Romeo and Juliet*, but I had paid no attention at all to *Pericles*, *Cymbeline*, and *Henry VIII*.

So I picked up copies of the scripts and checked out audio recordings of the plays from the library. For the next couple of weeks, I was immersed in obscure works by one of the world's best dramatic storytellers.

What did I learn? Well, *Timon of Athens* turned out to be an incredible dud, an encouraging sign that even the greats can have off days. I also got to discover that *The Winter's Tale* is one of the most charming plays I'd ever experienced.

My occasional forays into the classics have broadened my scope and made me a better storyteller. I know from personal experience that Dante may be more historically significant than narratively skilled. But I also know that Ovid is one of the most delightful writers of all time, and I'm pleased that his work influences mine.

Find a Workshop/Support Group: Writing is lonely isolated work. But a writer can't improve and grow without feedback, so you'd do well to find a group of like-minded people to help you.

The key to workshops I conduct is that the writers present their work to be read around the table. The writer does not actively participate in the reading because the object is to hear what he or she has written and to gauge how it's being received. The toughest part of this exercise is for the writers to simply hear their work without commenting or defending.

Did that joke you wrote get a laugh? Did your emotionally touching scene inspire unintended giggles? Is your point clear to the people around the table? Once a submission has been read aloud, I'll frequently ask one of the readers to simply synopsize the story. It's amazing how often the synopsis strays from what the writer meant.

This sort of visceral feedback is invaluable. It might be helpful to hear constructive criticism from other group members, but nothing they say will strike you as clearly as the effect your story has while it's being performed in the room.

As you hunt for a workshop, I'd urge you to find a group that speaks to your level. If you join a group of writers who are far more skilled than you, you simply won't be able to communicate effectively. Conversely, finding a group in which you are the star may flatter your ego, but it won't teach you much about improvements you must make.

Your ideal group posits you somewhere in the middle of the pack. You want some group members to be more experienced and skillful than you so you can measure your work against the standard they set. You want other members to be below your prowess. This not only gives your vanity a much-needed lift, it also urges you to crystallize (and even share) your storytelling secrets with your less-experienced colleagues.

A Hundred Plays in a Hundred Days: This is a pretty simple but challenging exercise gleaned from my years as a professional story analyst. Over the course of three or four months, I would have you read a hundred screenplays (an occasional book wouldn't hurt if that's your preference).

Once you have finished each script, I'd have you synopsize the reciprocal action of the story in no more than two or three pages. Obviously this sort of compression means that you'll omit a great deal of detail. That's the point because you'll need to find the spine of the story: the central character, the main conflict, the reciprocal actions, the beginning, middle and end.

I'd also have you synopsize the script in a single sentence. In industry terms, this is the "log line," the single idea around which the story is built. As you work on your own scripts, you'll see that knowing your log line is a vital procedural step.

What does this exercise accomplish? For one thing, it causes you to read screenplays, the form you are hoping to master. For another, it causes you to break down a screenplay into component parts so you can learn what those parts are and how they work.

After you do this exercise, you'll know something about screenplays that you don't currently know. I can't tell you what the full breadth of that knowledge is, but on some level, you'll come to see that *Citizen Kane* and *Toy Story* are exactly the same.

I'll get you started by adding a sample of Log Line and Synopsis of an early draft of Michael Arndt's *Little Miss Sunshine*. It should give you an idea of what you are looking to accomplish:

Title: *Little Miss Sunshine*

Author: Michael Arndt

> **Log Line:** An embattled family's future depends on their little daughter's performance in a children's beauty contest.
>
> **Synopsis:** SHERYL, 40, is under a lot of pressure. In addition to holding down a middle-management job, she's raising her undernourished, Mohawk-haired son DWAYNE, 15, her plump beauty contest wannabe daughter OLIVE, 7, and tending to her horny, heroin-snorting father-in-law GRANDPA, 80 (an exile from the old-age home). Now she must harbor her suicidally depressed brother FRANK. A semi-successful motivational speaker, second husband RICHARD, 45, isn't much help.
>
> Frank and Dwayne form a mild bond since the former is depressive and the latter refuses to talk because he hates everyone. The dinner table is a nightmare as Sheryl details Frank's latest suicide attempt. It seems that academician Frank lost his would-be gay lover and a major grant to rival scholar LARRY.
>
> The big news is that Olive is a state finalist for the Little Miss Sunshine contest. The family is so co-dependent that everyone has to make the long trek to the contest. It's a hell of a ride with Grandpa urging Dwayne to have as much sex as possible, Frank spouting meaningless arcana and Richard making Olive self-conscious about her

weight. It doesn't help that the car breaks down and must be continually push-started.

It gets worse. Richard is crushed to learn that promoter STAN won't take on Richard's new self-help book. Frank is embarrassed to run into rival Larry and would-be lover JOSH. The book failure puts the family in financial danger, and Sheryl is ready to dump Richard. Olive fears that she will lose Richard's love if she becomes a "loser" in the contest.

Richard abandons the family to unsuccessfully confront promoter Stan. Grandpa dies in his sleep. Sheryl prepares the family to deal with the onset of bankruptcy. But Richard returns and insists that the family needs a victory. They'll take Grandpa's corpse with them so that Olive can get to the contest in time.

A cop pulls the family over because of car trouble. He fails to spot Grandpa's corpse, but he salaciously confiscates Grandpa's porn magazines. Another trauma arises when Dwayne (who yearns to be a military pilot) suddenly discovers that he's color-blind — another dream shot to hell. Dwayne starts talking. In fact he fumes his hatred towards everyone in the family. Frank calms Dwayne and the family races to the contest deadline.

Using death-defying driving tactics, Richard delivers Olive to the contest at the last possible minute. Olive gets a look at the competition. If she were self-conscious, she'd lose all hope. Frank passes the time reading a newspaper only to see that rival Larry has published a hot new book that tops anything Frank's ever done. Dwayne settles back into morose silence. Richard arranges for Grandpa's cremation.

Olive is about to go onstage, and Richard pleads with her to come back victorious. While the contest gets underway,

Frank and Dwayne spend quiet time on the beach comparing notes about suicidal impulses. It seems to lighten both of them. Frank uses his arcane knowledge to give Dwayne a much-needed lift. Most importantly, they accept that they are "losers" and stop fighting it.

Meanwhile Richard loses heart when he sees Olive's competitors perform. There's no way his daughter can win. He wants to pull her from the contest so she won't be embarrassed. Sheryl is touched by Richard's unexpected vulnerability. Maybe it's something she can use to build a future with Richard.

Fortunately, Olive doesn't pay attention to this fear. She's worked out her dance routine with Grandpa's help, and it's mind-bogglingly nasty. The contest officials are appalled, but the family fights them off while Olive blows the audience away. By the end of the routine every member of the family is onstage, backing up Olive and dancing like maniacs.

Yeah, the family is facing bankruptcy and a long list of disasters. But when they're dancing, they can't be stopped.

So you now have a regimen. Like any workout routine, it only takes effect if you do it regularly. But if you do the work every day, you will transform yourself into something that you have never been before. I promise.

NOTE FROM VOGLER

Wish I'd thought of this. I wish I'd done it, five years ago — I'd be in much better shape professionally! Actually, I've done most of these things at some point, and some of them I've incorporated permanently into the pattern of my life. I keep a clip file of newspaper articles and images that I return to constantly for reference, inspiration, and story ideas. One of the most significant steps in my professional life has been aiming to write something every day, even it's only a few lines scribbled on a note pad or entered into the journal I keep in my computer. It may be fragments of a scene, notes for a story, or just an account of the day's activities, but it's built up my writing muscles and trained my nervous system to expect that every day I will do the physical activity of writing. I got the idea of doing these "daily pages" from a wonderful book called *The Artist's Way* by Julia Cameron which is a great guide to trusting and following the call of the artist's path. Another good source is *Writing Down the Bones: Freeing the Writer Within* by Natalie Goldberg. I heard her speak at a writers' conference one time and she made us all take out pencils and write something. She taught me that getting used to the physical act of writing or typing is as important to your professional life as the ideas you write.

CHAPTER TWENTY-SIX

What Studios Are
Looking For in a Script

 VOGLER

After reading a few thousand screenplays as a studio reader, I realized I was asking myself the same questions about each script over and over as I wrote my "coverage," the report in which I had to synopsize the story, describe its merits and problems, and make a recommendation. At some point I collected those recurring questions into a handout that I gave to my screenwriting and story analysis students. It's a checklist of questions that studio executives and their readers are asking themselves as they evaluate your screenplay, novel, or idea, but the same sort of questions determine the decisions of agents, book editors, directors, and actors when they read your work.

Many of these points will be obvious to a veteran or even a beginning writer, but storytelling is a complex activity and you soon find you can't remember everything all the time. So it can be useful to remind yourself now and then of the basics, and put yourself in the mindset of someone reading your story for the first time.

When I write scripts I find that the task breaks down into a series of steps that I call "passes," which are operations that you perform on the whole story to address specific issues, add levels, cut out unnecessary things, or bring a specific quality to it. For example, the first "pass" of a script is the first rough draft in which you plug in the major characters and situations, not worrying much about sub-plots and secondary characters. Then you might make a second "pass" over the whole script to improve those sub-plots, adding a few scenes or lines of dialogue to develop them and adding depth to the secondary characters. You might make another pass just to work on developing the villain, another to sharpen the dialogue or punch up the jokes, another to make sure the tone of the script is consistent, and so on. You'll probably make several passes just to edit out unnecessary bits, one of the best ways to improve any manuscript.

The questions in the following checklist suggest some of the operations that have to be performed. You may not need to make a formal "pass" over every page of your story to satisfy each of these items, but they all need to be considered in your writing process at some point.

CHARACTER

Are the characters believable?

Is their behavior consistent with human nature? Is it realistic? (Or, if it is a fantastic world where the rules are different, are the rules at least consistent and logical?)

Is character revealed through what people do (visually) rather than what they say? (Film is a visual medium; motion pictures are supposed to *move*.)

Is it clear who the story is about? Who are we cheering for?

Can you identify in some way with the main character (hero, anti-hero, protagonist)? Is he or she either likable and charming or "relatable," i.e., does he/she have some interesting flaw or problem that almost everyone can relate to?

Does the main character change, grow, develop or learn some life lesson?

Is the main character active rather than passive most of the time? If passive by nature, is there some point where she stands up for herself and switches to taking action?

Does he/she have both an inner and an outer problem to solve? Are the supporting characters good "foils" for the protagonist? Do they bring out hidden aspects of the protagonist or complement him with different qualities?

Are the hero and the antagonist evenly matched? Does the villain have some interesting advantages?

Does the story have appealing roles that top actors will be fighting to play?

STRUCTURE

Is it a good story? Is it compelling? Involving? Does it engage my emotions or stimulate the organs of my body? Does it make me *feel* something?

Is the conflict, or what the story is about, clear in the first few pages?

Does it flow? Or does it wear you out by being choppy and confusing?

Does it have strong narrative drive, moving forward with relentless energy? Does it avoid rambling and irrelevant tangents?

Does the story develop or unfold in an interesting, unpredictable way? Is something interesting or surprising happening every few minutes? (Hey, why not on every page?)

Is the opening exciting, grabbing the attention of the audience immediately with some surprise or mystery?

Are the scene transitions smooth or visually interesting?

Is the necessary exposition given in an elegant, offhand manner, avoiding blunt, clumsy revelation of plot details?

Does the story "get rolling" quickly enough?

Does the second act sustain your interest with fresh, unexpected developments?

Are major characters introduced early enough in the picture to establish a presence?

Does the climax pay off on the promise of the beginning?

Do the villains get their just comeuppance? Does the punishment fit the crime?

Does the writer "follow through" on all his story lines? Do minor characters work out their problems in ways that reflect the movie's theme?

Does the structure feel balanced, or is something missing, unnecessarily repeated, or in the wrong place?

Is the ending satisfying? Or does it leave you with that "So what?" feeling?

DIALOGUE

Does sound it the way really people talk?

Is it consistent? Do people stay "in character"?

Do all the characters sound different instead of all sounding like the writer's voice?

Is the dialogue appropriate to the time period or setting of the film?

If it's supposed to be a comedy, is it funny? (You'd be surprised how many comedy scripts aren't funny.)

Does the dialogue "track" well? That is, does one speech flow naturally into the next?

Is the script too "stagey" or "talky," relying too much on dialogue and not enough on visuals?

Are the speeches relatively short and easy for actors to memorize?

Does the main character (the Star?) have more lines (or better moments) than the other actors?

CONCEPT

Does it feel new or fresh? Or does it offer a new twist on something familiar?

Is there an audience for this? The ideal movie has something for everyone and appeals to all quadrants of the audience — young males, young females, older males and older females. A story that appeals to only one quadrant can succeed only if it brings out almost everyone in that segment; that is, has a very high "want-to-see" for that audience quadrant. It has to work harder to make its money.

Is there a strong central conflict reflecting different moralities or systems of belief, more than just good vs. evil?

Will the main idea of the film "grab" an audience? Is there a "hook"? Some threat, jeopardy, or mystery to involve the audience? Some sensation that gets people out of their chairs to see a movie?

Are there elements on which to build an advertising campaign? Something sensational to tease the audience with? Is it sexy or exciting in some way?

Is the idea unique? Does the movie offer something people can't see on TV every night?

Is it easily explained in a few words? Is it pitchable?

Is there a clear theme? Is it clear what this movie is about? Does every scene reflect on the central theme and introduce a new aspect of it?

Are there other films with similar qualities that can be used for comparison? Can it be capsulized in some form like "It's *Avatar* meets *Beverly Hills Chihuahua!*"?

Is the idea timely? Does it relate to something currently in the public awareness or in the "zeitgeist"? Does it evoke some universal fear or grant some universal wish?

If it's set in another time, is there some parallel to current events that will help the audience relate to it?

Is it cool?

BUDGET

Would the production be prohibitively expensive? (A cast of thousands, crowd scenes, exotic locales, remote time periods, lots of special effects, extensive underwater or nautical sequences, etc.) Does it have elements of strong universal appeal that will justify its high budget?

Does it have appeal for the world market, or does something about it limit its appeal down to one particular market and culture? Movies with a lot of dialogue may not play as well in other languages and sometimes highly verbal comedies or stories of national sports are not understood on the world stage. Epics, action, horror, and simple physical comedies travel further.

Are there any elements or scenes that could be cut to trim the budget? Can characters or scenes be combined to make a clearer, simpler story and save money?

Does the story depend on music rights or life rights that could be difficult or expensive to acquire?

Would "star" actors or other talent be required to make the project work? For example, would it only work in the hands of certain directors?

How have films with similar themes and budgets fared at the box office?

THE BOTTOM LINE

If you can only make ten movies a year, would this be one of them?

Is this a movie you, the studio executive, would go to see for your own enjoyment? Don't say yes to the project unless you would tell your family and everyone you know to see the picture without reservation.

Again, who is the intended audience for the film? Is that audience large enough to justify the cost of the picture? (Remember a film must make three or four times its production cost to show a profit, due to the high cost of prints and advertising.)

Does the script work on its own terms? It may be a schlocky exploitive horror movie, but is it a *good* schlocky exploitive horror movie?

Is it an appropriate project for the studio? Does it fit into the studio's general strategy for a balanced slate of pictures appealing to specific audiences? Is it what the studio management is looking for?

Is this a movie that has a good chance of being number one on its opening Friday night?

Keep these questions in mind as you compose your story, and go over the checklist one more time before you send out your manuscript. If you can't give a good answer to most of these questions, back to the drawing board!

CHAPTER TWENTY-SEVEN

FARE THEE WELL:
MY PARTING SHOT

—— VOGLER ——

When I was a kid growing up in the suburbs of St. Louis, family gatherings like Thanksgiving and the Fourth of July tended to break down into two separate camps. The womenfolk occupied the kitchen and dining room, preparing the food, playing Yahtzee, comparing recipes, and exchanging family stories. The men, my father and his many brothers, were congregated out in the garage or under a sun umbrella in the back yard, quaffing the local ale and talking about sports and their jobs, but mostly reminiscing about great power tools they had known. "Remember that band saw we had in the basement?" Uncle Fred would begin a typical reverie. "Oh yeah, that was a monster," replied Uncle Timer, "I almost lost my thumb on that one. Remember how Pop was cussing when we got stuck bringing it down the stairs?" That would remind another uncle of the pile of shovels that used to sit in a corner of the garage, recovered from various worksites, and how Pop, my father's father, would hand them out like candy to anyone who passed by.

My Dad and his brothers were all skilled tradesmen in the post-war construction industry, dependent on the tools they used every day of their working lives, and rather fond of them. The tools became associated with certain times in their lives, reminders of their labors and the stages of life they had been through. When my father, a cement mason, passed away, my sisters and I placed two things with him in his casket; a golf ball so he would always be ready to play, and one of his trowels, a diamond-shaped metal blade that he used to form and smooth the concrete. In his hands, that trowel could make concrete dance. His brother Warren noticed us putting the trowel near Dad's hand and put up a mild objection. "That's a good new pointing trowel," he said, but he understood our gesture and let it stay in the casket. In life, my father had a fascination with old tools, and in his retirement he liked to find and restore antique handsaws because they were beautiful objects, and besides, you could play tunes on them, flexing them against your knee and bowing them like a violin.

And that's our intention with this collection of tools for crafting stories, to resurrect and restore some of these time-worn implements so that you can use them in your work, and maybe even make music with them. Use them to make your stories dance and sing.

In offering up this inventory of tools we are aware that we are standing on the shoulders of many great teachers and master storytellers. We hope we have honored their tradition by bringing some attention to forgotten areas, and perhaps have made some small contribution to the body of knowledge.

We hope you've found something useful in our review of the processes and systems that we have collected in this kit. We find them more than useful; in fact, they are absolutely essential life-savers. They gave us compasses and maps to navigate our way through the thousands of stories we've had to absorb and respond to, and tools to shape and guide them. We also found a certain delight and pleasure in handling these tools, and we share an enthusiasm for them. We both had a genuine desire to share these things and stir up more conversation and discourse about them.

We hand off the tool kit and the discussion to you, to build on these approaches, to refine them and make them your own. By all means challenge them. You'll bring your own experiences and needs into the stream and you'll make your own discoveries in the archives of storytelling. The discussion that began with Aristotle and Theophrastus will go on and you will have your part in it. While many story tools are timeless and unchanging, our very idea of what stories are will continue to evolve as we bend and stretch them to fit new media or fill new human needs. We encourage you to make the tool kit your own and add new equipment to it as required.

We hope too that the quest will help you figure out why you're here and what you're supposed to do with your story-telling urges. Some of these ideas may cause you to vibrate at a higher frequency, exciting your imagination or making you eager to put them into practice. These are signals from your unconscious. Follow those leads; they are sources of power for you and will lead to new discoveries.

One thing is certain — you will get out of it what you put into it. In fact, we'll go one further, you'll get *more* out of it than you put in. We've found that when we actually apply these concepts and tools to something we're working on, a story we're writing, a movie we're analyzing or editing, a play we're directing, far more energy is released than we have put into it. We learn more than we thought possible, and the effect on the work, and on the audience, is greater than we had imagined.

So we wish you well, hoping you will use these tools for the greater good and enjoyment of all. In the words of engineer William Mulholland, when he opened the aqueduct that made modern Los Angeles possible, "There it is, take it."

Vogler and McKenna on one of their journeys.

ABOUT THE AUTHORS

 VOGLER

CHRISTOPHER VOGLER is a story consultant and the author of *The Writer's Journey: Mythic Structure for Writers*. He advises major Hollywood studios and talent on their stories and presents workshops on mythic structure for Fortune 500 companies and for audiences around the world. He wrote the screenplay for the animated feature *Jester Till* and was executive producer of the independent film *P.S. Your Cat Is Dead*.

Website: *www.thewritersjourney.com*
Blog: *http://chrisvogler@wordpress.com*
Email: *vogler.christopher@gmail.com*

 McKENNA

Trained as a theatre director, DAVID McKENNA has staged over one hundred plays, many of which were writer collaborations on new scripts. He has taught film courses for twenty years, notably at Columbia University, Barnard College and NYU. He has written story analysis on more than ten thousand scripts for private clients as well as for Focus Features, HBO and 20th Century-Fox. Contact David at *d1mck1@earthlink.net*.

THE WRITER'S JOURNEY - 3RD EDITION
MYTHIC STRUCTURE FOR WRITERS

CHRISTOPHER VOGLER

BEST SELLER

See why this book has become an international best seller and a true classic. *The Writer's Journey* explores the powerful relationship between mythology and storytelling in a clear, concise style that's made it required reading for movie executives, screenwriters, playwrights, scholars, and fans of pop culture all over the world.

Both fiction and nonfiction writers will discover a set of useful myth-inspired storytelling paradigms (i.e., "The Hero's Journey") and step-by-step guidelines to plot and character development. Based on the work of Joseph Campbell, *The Writer's Journey* is a must for all writers interested in further developing their craft.

The updated and revised third edition provides new insights and observations from Vogler's ongoing work on mythology's influence on stories, movies, and man himself.

"This book is like having the smartest person in the story meeting come home with you and whisper what to do in your ear as you write a screenplay. Insight for insight, step for step, Chris Vogler takes us through the process of connecting theme to story and making a script come alive."
> – Lynda Obst, Producer, *Sleepless in Seattle*, *How to Lose a Guy in 10 Days*;
> Author, *Hello, He Lied*

"This is a book about the stories we write, and perhaps more importantly, the stories we live. It is the most influential work I have yet encountered on the art, nature, and the very purpose of storytelling."
> – Bruce Joel Rubin, Screenwriter, *Stuart Little 2*, *Deep Impact*,
> *Ghost*, *Jacob's Ladder*

CHRISTOPHER VOGLER is a veteran story consultant for major Hollywood film companies and a respected teacher of filmmakers and writers around the globe. He has influenced the stories of movies from *The Lion King* to *Fight Club* to *The Thin Red Line* and most recently wrote the first installment of *Ravenskull*, a Japanese-style manga or graphic novel. He is the executive producer of the feature film *P.S. Your Cat is Dead* and writer of the animated feature *Jester Till*.

$26.95 · 448 PAGES · ORDER NUMBER 76RLS · ISBN: 9781932907360

CINEMATIC STORYTELLING
THE 100 MOST POWERFUL FILM CONVENTIONS
EVERY FILMMAKER MUST KNOW

CINEMATIC STORYTELLING

THE 100 MOST POWERFUL FILM CONVENTIONS EVERY FILMMAKER MUST KNOW JENNIFER VAN SIJLL

JENNIFER VAN SIJLL

BEST SELLER

How do directors use screen direction to suggest conflict? How do screenwriters exploit film space to show change? How does editing style determine emotional response?

Many first-time writers and directors do not ask these questions. They forego the huge creative resource of the film medium, defaulting to dialog to tell their screen story. Yet most movies are carried by sound and picture. The industry's most successful writers and directors have mastered the cinematic conventions specific to the medium. They have harnessed non-dialog techniques to create some of the most cinematic moments in movie history.

This book is intended to help writers and directors more fully exploit the medium's inherent storytelling devices. It contains 100 non-dialog techniques that have been used by the industry's top writers and directors. From *Metropolis* and *Citizen Kane* to *Dead Man* and *Kill Bill*, the book illustrates – through 500 frame grabs and 75 script excerpts – how the inherent storytelling devices specific to film were exploited.

You will learn:
· How non-dialog film techniques can advance story.
· How master screenwriters exploit cinematic conventions to create powerful scenarios.

"Cinematic Storytelling *scores a direct hit in terms of concise information and perfectly chosen visuals, and it also searches out... and finds... an emotional core that many books of this nature either miss or are afraid of.*"
> — Kirsten Sheridan, Director, *Disco Pigs*; Co-writer, *In America*

"*Here is a uniquely fresh, accessible, and truly original contribution to the field. Jennifer van Sijll takes her readers in a wholly new direction, integrating aspects of screenwriting with all the film crafts in a way I've never before seen. It is essential reading not only for screenwriters but also for filmmakers of every stripe.*"
> — Prof. Richard Walter, UCLA Screenwriting Chairman

JENNIFER VAN SIJLL has taught film production, film history, and screenwriting. She is currently on the faculty at San Francisco State's Department of Cinema.

$24.95 · 230 PAGES · ORDER NUMBER 35RLS · ISBN: 9781932907056

DIRECTING ACTORS
CREATING MEMORABLE PERFORMANCES
FOR FILM AND TELEVISION

JUDITH WESTON

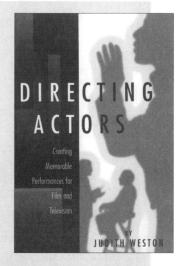

BEST SELLER

Directing film or television is a high-stakes occupation. It captures your full attention at every moment, calling on you to commit every resource and stretch yourself to the limit. It's the white-water rafting of entertainment jobs. But for many directors, the excitement they feel about a new project tightens into anxiety when it comes to working with actors.

This book provides a method for establishing creative, collaborative relationships with actors, getting the most out of rehearsals, troubleshooting poor performances, giving briefer directions, and much more. It addresses what actors want from a director, what directors do wrong, and constructively analyzes the director-actor relationship.

"Judith Weston is an extraordinarily gifted teacher."
> – David Chase, Emmy® Award-Winning Writer,
> Director, and Producer *The Sopranos,*
> *Northern Exposure, I'll Fly Away*

"I believe that working with Judith's ideas and principles has been the most useful time I've spent preparing for my work. I think that if Judith's book were mandatory reading for all directors, the quality of the director-actor process would be transformed, and better drama would result."
> – John Patterson, Director
> *Six Feet Under, CSI: Crime Scene Investigation,*
> *The Practice, Law and Order*

"I know a great teacher when I find one! Everything in this book is brilliant and original and true."
> – Polly Platt, Producer, *Bottle Rocket*
> Executive Producer, *Broadcast News, The War of the Roses*

JUDITH WESTON was a professional actor for 20 years and has taught Acting for Directors for over a decade.

$26.95 · 314 PAGES · ORDER NUMBER 4RLS · ISBN: 9780941188241

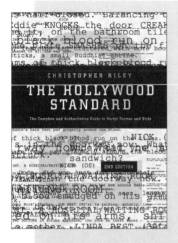

THE HOLLYWOOD STANDARD
2ND EDITION
THE COMPLETE AND AUTHORITATIVE GUIDE TO SCRIPT FORMAT AND STYLE

CHRISTOPHER RILEY

This is the book screenwriter Antwone Fisher (*Antwone Fisher, Tales from the Script*) insists his writing students at UCLA read. This book convinced John August (*Big Fish, Charlie and the Chocolate Factory*) to stop dispensing formatting advice on his popular writing website. His new advice: Consult *The Hollywood Standard*. The book working and aspiring writers keep beside their keyboards and rely on every day. Written by a professional screenwriter whose day job was running the vaunted script shop at Warner Bros., this book is used at USC's School of Cinema, UCLA, and the acclaimed Act One Writing Program in Hollywood, and in screenwriting programs around the world. It is the definitive guide to script format.

The Hollywood Standard describes in clear, vivid prose and hundreds of examples how to format every element of a screenplay or television script. A reference for everyone who writes for the screen, from the novice to the veteran, this is the dictionary of script format, with instructions for formatting everything from the simplest master scene heading to the most complex and challenging musical underwater dream sequence. This new edition includes a quick start guide, plus new chapters on avoiding a dozen deadly formatting mistakes, clarifying the difference between a spec script and production script, and mastering the vital art of proofreading. For the first time, readers will find instructions for formatting instant messages, text messages, email exchanges and caller ID.

"Aspiring writers sometimes wonder why people don't want to read their scripts. Sometimes it's not their story. Sometimes the format distracts. To write a screenplay, you need to learn the science. And this is the best, simplest, easiest to read book to teach you that science. It's the one I recommend to my students at UCLA."

— Antwone Fisher, from the foreword

CHRISTOPHER RILEY is a professional screenwriter working in Hollywood with his wife and writing partner, Kathleen Riley. Together they wrote the 1999 theatrical feature *After the Truth*, a multiple-award-winning German language courtroom thriller. Since then, the husband-wife team has written scripts ranging from legal and political thrillers to action-romances for Touchstone Pictures, Paramount Pictures, Mandalay Television Pictures and Sean Connery's Fountainbridge Films.

In addition to writing, the Rileys train aspiring screenwriters for work in Hollywood and have taught in Los Angeles, Chicago, Washington D.C., New York, and Paris. From 2005 to 2008, the author directed the acclaimed Act One Writing Program in Hollywood.

$24.95 · 208 PAGES · ORDER NUMBER 130RLS · ISBN: 9781932907636

MYTH AND THE MOVIES
DISCOVERING THE MYTHIC STRUCTURE
OF 50 UNFORGETTABLE FILMS

STUART VOYTILLA

FOREWORD BY CHRISTOPHER VOGLER
AUTHOR OF *THE WRITER'S JOURNEY*

An illuminating companion piece to *The Writer's Journey*, *Myth and the Movies* applies the mythic structure Vogler developed to 50 well-loved U.S. and foreign films. This comprehensive book offers a greater understanding of why some films continue to touch and connect with audiences generation after generation.

Movies discussed include *The Godfather*, *Some Like It Hot*, *Citizen Kane*, *Halloween*, *Jaws*, *Annie Hall*, *Chinatown*, *The Fugitive*, *Sleepless in Seattle*, *The Graduate*, *Dances with Wolves*, *Beauty and the Beast*, *Platoon*, and *Die Hard*.

"Stuart Voytilla's Myth and the Movies *is a remarkable achievement: an ambitious, thought-provoking, and cogent analysis of the mythic underpinnings of fifty great movies. It should prove a valuable resource for film teachers, students, critics, and especially screenwriters themselves, whose challenge, as Voytilla so clearly understands, is to constantly reinvent a mythology for our times."*

> — Ted Tally, Academy Award® Screenwriter, *Silence of the Lambs*

"Myth and the Movies is a must for every writer who wants to tell better stories. Voytilla guides his readers to a richer and deeper understanding not only of mythic structure, but also of the movies we love."

> — Christopher Wehner, Web editor,
> *The Screenwriters Utopia* and *Creative Screenwriting*

"I've script consulted for ten years and I've studied every genre thoroughly. I thought I knew all their nuances - until I read Voytilla's book. This ones goes on my Recommended Reading List. A fascinating analysis of the Hero's Myth for all genres."

> — Lou Grantt, *Hollywood Scriptwriter* Magazine

STUART VOYTILLA is a screenwriter, literary consultant, teacher, and author of *Writing the Comedy Film*.

$26.95 · 300 PAGES · ORDER NUMBER 39RLS · ISBN: 9780941188661

24 HOURS | **1.800.833.5738** | **WWW.MWP.COM**

SAVE THE CAT!®
THE LAST BOOK ON SCREENWRITING YOU'LL EVER NEED!

BLAKE SNYDER

BLAKE SNYDER

BEST SELLER

He's made millions of dollars selling screenplays to Hollywood and now screenwriter Blake Snyder tells all. "Save the Cat!®" is just one of Snyder's many ironclad rules for making your ideas more marketable and your script more satisfying – and saleable, including:
- The four elements of every winning logline.
- The seven immutable laws of screenplay physics.
- The 10 genres and why they're important to your movie.
- Why your Hero must serve your idea.
- Mastering the Beats.
- Mastering the Board to create the Perfect Beast.
- How to get back on track with ironclad and proven rules for script repair.

This ultimate insider's guide reveals the secrets that none dare admit, told by a show biz veteran who's proven that you can sell your script if you can save the cat.

"Imagine what would happen in a town where more writers approached screenwriting the way Blake suggests? My weekend read would dramatically improve, both in sellable/producible content and in discovering new writers who understand the craft of storytelling and can be hired on assignment for ideas we already have in house."
> – From the Foreword by Sheila Hanahan Taylor, Vice President,Development at Zide/Perry Entertainment, whose films include *American Pie, Cats and Dogs, Final Destination*

"One of the most comprehensive and insightful how-to's out there. Save the Cat!® is a must-read for both the novice and the professional screenwriter."
> – Todd Black, Producer, *The Pursuit of Happyness, The Weather Man, S.W.A.T, Alex and Emma, Antwone Fisher*

"Want to know how to be a successful writer in Hollywood? The answers are here. Blake Snyder has written an insider's book that's informative – and funny, too."
> – David Hoberman, Producer, *The Shaggy Dog* (2005), *Raising Helen, Walking Tall, Bringing Down the House, Monk* (TV)

BLAKE SNYDER, besides selling million-dollar scripts to both Disney and Spielberg, was one of Hollywood's most successful spec screenwriters. Blake's vision continues on *www.blakesnyder.com*.

$19.95 · 216 PAGES · ORDER NUMBER 34RLS · ISBN: 9781932907001

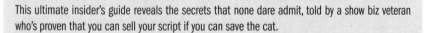

SELLING YOUR STORY IN 60 SECONDS
THE GUARANTEED WAY TO GET
YOUR SCREENPLAY OR NOVEL READ

MICHAEL HAUGE

BEST SELLER

Best-selling author Michael Hauge reveals:
- How to Design, Practice, and Present the
  60-Second Pitch
- The Cardinal Rule of Pitching
- The 10 Key Components of a Commercial Story
- The 8 Steps to a Powerful Pitch
- Targeting Your Buyers
- Securing Opportunities to Pitch
- Pitching Templates
- And much more, including "The Best Pitch I Ever Heard," an exclusive collection
  from major film executives

"Michael Hauge's principles and methods are so well argued that the mysteries of effective screenwriting can be understood — even by directors."

— Phillip Noyce, Director, *Patriot Games, Clear and Present Danger,*
The Quiet American, Rabbit-Proof Fence

"... one of the few authentically good teachers out there. Every time I revisit my notes, I learn something new or reinforce something that I need to remember."

— Jeff Arch, Screenwriter, *Sleepless in Seattle, Iron Will*

"Michael Hauge's method is magic — but unlike most magicians, he shows you how the trick is done."

— William Link, Screenwriter & Co-Creator, *Columbo; Murder, She Wrote*

"By following the formula we learned in Michael Hauge's seminar, we got an agent, optioned our script, and now have a three-picture deal at Disney."

— Paul Hoppe and David Henry, Screenwriters

MICHAEL HAUGE is the author of *Writing Screenplays That Sell*, now in its 30th printing, and has presented his seminars and lectures to more than 30,000 writers and filmmakers. He has coached hundreds of screenwriters and producers on their screenplays and pitches, and has consulted on projects for Warner Brothers, Disney, New Line, CBS, Lifetime, Julia Roberts, Jennifer Lopez, Kirsten Dunst, and Morgan Freeman.

$12.95 · 150 PAGES · ORDER NUMBER 64RLS · ISBN: 9781932907209

24 HOURS | **1.800.833.5738** | WWW.MWP.COM

{ THE MYTH OF MWP }

In a dark time, a light bringer came along, leading the curious and the frustrated to clarity and empowerment. It took the well-guarded secrets out of the hands of the few and made them available to all. It spread a spirit of openness and creative freedom, and built a storehouse of knowledge dedicated to the betterment of the arts.

The essence of the Michael Wiese Productions (MWP) is empowering people who have the burning desire to express themselves creatively. We help them realize their dreams by putting the tools in their hands. We demystify the sometimes secretive worlds of screenwriting, directing, acting, producing, film financing, and other media crafts.

By doing so, we hope to bring forth a realization of 'conscious media' which we define as being positively charged, emphasizing hope and affirming positive values like trust, cooperation, self-empowerment, freedom, and love. Grounded in the deep roots of myth, it aims to be healing both for those who make the art and those who encounter it. It hopes to be transformative for people, opening doors to new possibilities and pulling back veils to reveal hidden worlds.

MWP has built a storehouse of knowledge unequaled in the world, for no other publisher has so many titles on the media arts. Please visit www.mwp.com where you will find many free resources and a 25% discount on our books. Sign up and become part of the wider creative community!

Onward and upward,

Michael Wiese
Publisher/Filmmaker